PHILIP TERRY

Dante's Inferno

D1629499

CARCANET

First published in Great Britain in 2014 by
Carcanet Press Limited
Alliance House
Cross Street
Manchester M2 7AQ

www.carcanet.co.uk

Copyright © Philip Terry 2014

The right of Philip Terry to be identified as the author of this work
has been asserted by him in accordance with the
Copyright, Designs and Patents Act of 1988
All rights reserved

This is a work of fiction.

A CIP catalogue record for this book is available from the British Library

ISBN 978 1 84777 220 6

The publisher acknowledges financial assistance from Arts Council England

Typeset by XL Publishing Services, Exmouth
Printed and bound in England by SRP Ltd, Exeter

ACKNOWLEDGEMENTS

Thanks to Tim Atkins, Mark Burnhope, Adrian Clarke, Sarah Crewe, James Davies, Steven Fowler, Ulli Freer, Jesse Glass, Peter Hughes, Piers Hugill, Tom Jencks, Peter Kennedy, Sophie Mayer, Aodán McCardle, Stephen Mooney, William Rowe, Michael Schmidt and Scott Thurston, who have previously published sections from this sequence, usually in a different form, in books, pamphlets and magazines.

I would also like to thank Ann Davey and Lou Terry, who have lived through this, as well as all the friends and poets who have helped this work along in one way or another with suggestions, encouragement, and opportunities to read, in particular Wayne Clements, Lyndon Davies, Cristina Fumagalli, John Goodby, Seamus Heaney, Jeff Hilson, Keith Jebb, Antony John, Jess Kenny, Matt Martin, Harry Mathews, Adrian May, David Miller, Marjorie Perloff, Tom Raworth, Stephen Rodefer, Tony Tackling, Jonathan White and Johan de Wit. Without the enthusiasm and support of all of these individuals this book would never have been written. Finally, I would like to thank Robert Sheppard for supplying some of the villains for Canto XIX.

For Marina Warner

CONTENTS

CANTO I

Halfway through a bad trip
I found myself in this stinking car park,
Underground, miles from Amarillo.

Students in thongs stood there,
Eating junk food from skips,
     flagmen spewing E's,

Their breath of fetid
Myrrh and ratsbane,
    doners

And condemned chicken shin
    rose like
         distemper.

Then I retched on rising ground;
Rabbits without ears, faces eaten away
       by myxomatosis

Crawled towards a bleak lake
    to drink
        of leucotomy.

The stink would revive a
    sparrow, spreadeagled on
    a lectern.

It so horrified my heart
    I shat
       botox.

Here, by the toxic water,
    lay a spotted trout, its glow
    lighting paths for the VC.

And nigh the bins a giant rat,
Seediness oozing from her Flemish pores,
Pushed me backwards, bit by bit

Into Square 5,
>   where the wind gnaws
>   and sunshine is spent.

By the cashpoint
>   a bum asked for a light,
>   hoarse from long silence, beaming.

When I saw him gyrate,
His teeth all wasted,
>   natch,

His eyes
>   long dead
>   through speed and booze,

I cried out
>   'Take pity,
Whatever you are, man or ghost!'

'Not man, though formerly a man,'
>   he says, 'I hail from Providence,
>   Rhode Island, a Korean vet.

Once I was a poet, I wrote
>   of bean spasms,
>   was anthologised in *Fuck You*.'

'You're never Berrigan, that spring
Where all the river of style freezes?'
I ask, awe all over my facials.

'I'm an American
>   Primitive,' he says,
'I make up each verse as it comes,

By putting things
>   where they
>   have to go.'

'O glory of every poet, have a light,
May my Zippo benefit me now,
And all my stripping of your *Sonnets*.

You see this hairy she-rat
            that stalks me like a pimp:
Get her   off my back,

            for every vein and pulse
Throughout my frame she hath
                        made quake.'

'You must needs another way pursue,'
He says, winking while I shade my pin,
'If you wouldst 'scape this beast.

Come, she lets none past her,
Save the VC; if she breathes on you,
                        you're teaching nights.

This way, freshman, come,
If I'm not far wrong we can find
A bar, and talk it over with Ed and Tom.'

I went where he led, across a square
And down some steps,
                        following the crowd.

The SU bar, where we queued
For 30 minutes
To get a watery beer, was packed;

                        Ed and Tom
Sat at a banquette in the corner
Chain-smoking and swapping jokes.

Here we joined them,
                        till closing time,
                        the beer doing the talking.

'Look,' said Tom, 'if this guy's got funding
And approval from the Dean and whatever,
Why not take him round?'

'Show him the works,' said Ed, 'no holds barred!'
'You mean,' said Berrigan, 'give him
                        a campus tour,

Like, give him Hell?'
'That's exactly what I mean,' said Ed.
'Let's drink to it!' said Tom,

At which we all raised our glasses,
Unsteadily, clinking them together above
The full ashtray.

'Hell,' pronounced Berrigan gnomically,
'Is other people. Sartre said that.
Hell is Hell. I said that.'

Now people were leaving,
                            we shifted outside,
Into the cold air,

Where we lingered a moment sharing a last
Cigarette, then split,
                    Ed and Tom going to their digs

Leaving me and Ted to breathe the night air.

CANTO II

The day was dying,
    the rabbits, unable to move,
    sat confused in the fading light,

And I too found myself stuck to the spot
    as I do
        now,

At the thought of that terrible journey
Which outdoes memory.
Now, Oulipo, come to my aid,

And muses, if you are there, now
Is the moment to show yourselves,
As I inscribe what I saw.

'Poet,' I said, 'who come to guide me,
Do you think I'm cut out for this?
In *Memorial Day* you said you

    "heard the dead, the city dead
The devils that surround us,"
And in life you always had one foot

In the underworld – and I don't just mean
You were friends with Lou Reed
        and Drella.

Like Virgil, who wrote of Sylvius'
    father, who, while subject to corruption,
    journeyed to the immortal world,

You have that special power
    to penetrate the veil of sense;
    but *I'm* no Aeneas.

Nor am I a Heaney or a Walcott,
Come to mention it,
By what right should *I* go?

Perhaps you've got the wrong man?
And then, if I say I'm up for it,
I fear I might make a fool of myself.

You see what I'm driving at –
Perhaps you can understand my
                                    dilemma.'

'I get your drift,' said Berrigan, 'you're
Getting what in the trade we call cold feet.
You've got that

                          fear that all too often
Turns a man away from a noble enterprise,
As a frightened beast that runs from its own shadow.

Now listen up. I'll tell you why I came
And why I first took pity on your
                                    plight.

I was hanging out among those souls in Limbo
When a Lady came up to me
And dragged me out of my lethargy.

She was so fair and blessed
That I was won over at once.
Her eyes shone with a light brighter than any

Eye-liner, and she began in soft and gentle
Yet commanding words to address me,
With the voice of an angel:

"Oh noble spirit, courteous Rhode Islander,
You who taught in the Poetry Project
At St Mark's, and indeed taught here too,

Whose fame still shines resplendent in the world
And will continue to shine as long as Time lasts,
I have a friend and colleague, so impeded

In his way across the Essex wastes
                    that he has turned back for
                                    sheer terror,

6

And I fear already
From what I have heard in London,
That I have come too late for his relief.

Now go, and with your ready turn of phrase,
And all the art at your disposal,
Help him, so that I may have solace.

I who urge you to go am Marina;
I come from a place I must quickly return to,
For I need to give a talk at the

British Library, this same afternoon,
Where there is a symposium on the sonnet,
With Jeff Hilson and Paul Muldoon –

When I return there, often will I sing your praise."
She was silent then, so I began:
"Oh Lady of Grace, aren't you that

Lady writer on the TV
Talking about the Virgin Mary
Celebrated in that Dire Straits song?

It's good to meet you ma'am, and let me
Tell you now, you can rely on me to
Get the job done. It'll be a pleasure,

And a good excuse to get out of this place,
Which gets real dull at times.
But tell me, what madness

Brought you to this point of spacelessness,
Stuck out here in the marshlands of Essex,
And away from your spacious home in town?"

"That song," she replied, "is not really about me –
It's a *chanson d'amour* about a beloved
Of Mark Knopfler's, of whom I briefly remind him.

As for your other question, why I fear not
To come within this place,
I can answer with ease:

A woman only stands in fear of those things
That have the power to do us harm,
Of nothing else, for nothing else is fearful.

I first heard tell of my friend's predicament
On a lunch date with Dawn and Michèle,
And they urged me to make this untimely visit;

There never was an entrepreneur in all of Texas
More anxious to pursue his selfish ends
Than I was, having heard this,

To rush down here and do what I could,
Confiding in thy noble speech, which honours thee,
And they who have heard it!"

After telling me all this, she turned away
Her bright eyes, weeping, then made her way
To the car park.

To cut a long story short, that's why I
Came to get you, just in time to stop that
Giant rat getting its teeth into you.

So what's your problem?
Why chicken out now, with dames like these
To look out for you?

Pull yourself together, there's not a moment
To lose.'
              As daffodils, bent down and cowed

By the chill night air, lift themselves up
And open
                when the sun whitens them,

So my courage began to come back,
And I stood up,
                as one who is ready to go.

'I was a fool to doubt you,' I said,
'Let's get moving.'
These are the words I spoke, and as Berrigan turned,

I entered on the savage path.

CANTO III

THROUGH ME THE WAY TO THE DOLEFUL CAMPUS,
THROUGH ME THE WAY TO ETERNAL DEBT,
THROUGH ME THE WAY TO THE FORSAKEN GENERATION.

FREEDOM OF THOUGHT INSPIRED MY FOUNDERS;
POLITICAL EXPEDIENCY RUINED ME,
COUPLED BY BETRAYAL OF PRINCIPLE AND PLEDGE.

BEFORE ME NOTHING BUT ETERNAL THINGS
WERE MADE, NOW I SHALL MARK YOU ETERNALLY.
ABANDON ALL HOPE, YOU WHO ENTER HERE.

I saw these words spelled out on a digital display
Above the entrance to the Knowledge Gateway.
'Master,' I said, 'this is scary.'

He answered me, speaking with a drawl:
'Now you need to grit your teeth,
This isn't the moment to shit yourself.

We're at the spot I spoke about
Where you will see souls in pain
Who perverted the good of intellect.'

Placing his hand on my shoulder, and flashing
Me a smile, though not one that reassured me,
He led me in.

Here groans and cries and shrieks of grief
Echoed through the freezing fog
And made me weep with fear;

A confusion of tongues,
Greek, Polish, Arabic, German, Dutch,
Strained with notes of tortured woe,

Rose into the sightless air,
Like frenzied seagulls
                          at a landfill site.

And I: 'What's this
                          noise I hear?
Who are all these tortured by grief?'

And Berrigan replied: 'They are surfers,
Dudes who coasted through life, drifting in and out
Of degrees and jobs without conviction.

They are mixed with those repulsive civil servants
Neither faithful nor unfaithful to their leaders,
Whose love was all for self.

Oxbridge, to keep its reputation, annulled
Their degrees, and even Essex
                          would not honour them.'

'Master,' I asked, 'what's eating them?
Why are they making such a racket?'
'That,' he says, 'I can tell you in a nutshell.

They have no hope of death
Yet the life they lead is so low
That they envy all the other shades.

Nobody on earth will remember them;
Funding bodies dismiss them out of hand.
Let's not talk about it: look and walk on.'

And as I looked I saw in the gloom
A giant screen, and on it the giant mouth
Of a talent show host, a man called Callow,

If I caught it right; in front of the screen
Such a crowd had gathered, I wondered
How death could have undone so many.

A few of these tortured souls I recognised,
Among them a couple of red-heads:
One who had amassed a few credits

In Philosophy and Literature before
Drifting into telecommunications sales,
Another who had been unable to choose

Between poetry and stand-up.
These wretches were stripped naked
And picked on by wasps and hornets

Which buzzed in their ears
And made their swollen faces run with blood
And pus, where fat maggots fed.

When I looked away from this awful sight
I saw another crowd queuing by the bank
Of a swamp which had formed in a building site.

                    'Master,' I asked,
'Are these more students? What makes them
So eager to make the crossing?'

And Berrigan, my guide, replied:
'Hold your horses, you'll see
                    soon enough.'

And I, biting my lip,
Said nothing more,
            until we reached the muddy shore.

Then suddenly, coming towards us in a bark,
An old man, hoary white with eld,
Bellowed: 'Woe to you, wicked students! Hope not

Ever to see a grant again. I come to take
You to the main campus
Into eternal loans, there to dwell

In sticky heat and dry-ice. And thou, who there
Standest, live spirit! Get thee hence, and leave
These who are dead.' And when he saw I didn't

Budge, he added: 'By other way
Shalt thou come ashore, not by this passage.
Thee a nimbler boat must carry.'

Then Berrigan spoke slowly: 'This is no time to get
Imperious, Dr May, it is willed by Senate,
That is all you need to know. Step aside.'

His words brought silence to the woolly cheeks
Of the boatman guarding the muddy swamp,
Whose eyes glowed like burning coals.

But all the students, shagged out and naked,
Grew pale, and their teeth began to chatter,
At the pronouncement they'd heard.

They cursed the day they were born, they
Cursed the coalition, they cursed their fathers
For not having vasectomies.

Then, like lost souls, wailing bitterly,
They squelched knee-deep in mud, towards
The shore of the forsaken building site.

Dr May called them together with his
Ferryman's song, and with his oar he walloped the
Latecomers, saying: 'Put that on your SACS forms!'

As at the start of the Autumn term,
When the leaves begin to fall,
Covering the ground with a slippery carpet,

So did the doomed freshers
Drop from that shore into the bark,
Lured by the siren song.

Off they go across the swamp waters,
And before they reach the opposite shore
A new crowd gathers on this side.

'My friend,' Berrigan said to me then,
'Everyone who wants to get a degree
Gathers here, from all corners of the globe;

They want to cross the swamp, they are eager;
It is the fear of being left on the
Scrapheap that urges them on

Into debt and toil and hardship;
Only a fool would follow, so if Dr May
Warns you off, you see what he's saying.'

As he finished, the ground shook with a violent
Tremor, as the Wivenhoe fault opened
Anew in the Palaeozoic rocks.

A whirlwind burst out of the cracked earth,
A wind that crackled like an electric storm;
It struck my body like a cattle prod

And as a man in Guantanamo Bay, I fell.

CANTO IV

The crack of fiercely hit squash balls
Woke me from my blackout so that I started
Like one woken from a deep sleep

Or like some unfortunate commuter
Rising to the call of alarm–clock Britain;
Once on my feet I steadied myself

And saw from an illuminated sign
That I had been borne to a place called
Valley, though it more resembled a ditch;

The place thundered with endless wailing
Which issued from the Sports Hall, but when I
Put my face to the glass, I discerned nothing,

For it was all steamed up with sweat;
'It's time to begin our descent into the
Blind world below,' said Berrigan, his face

All pale, and I, who saw his complexion,
For even his beard could not hide it, asked
'How will I cope, when even you're afraid,

Who art wont to be my strength in doubt?'
And he spoke back: 'It's the misery of the
Fuck-ups here below which paints my face with

That pity which you mistake for fear;
Though I walk through the Valley of the Shadow
Of Death, I shall fear no evil – for I am

A lot more insane than this Valley.
Now, let's get moving, the journey is long.'
He stepped forward then, leading the way for me,

Towards our next port of call. As we advanced
Along a straight track, no wailing could be heard,
Only the sound of sighs coming from

A vast car park, where none of the vehicles
Could be moved for all had been clamped,
Sighs that rose from grief without torment.

Berrigan then said: 'If you want to know
What kind of souls these are that surround you,
I'll let you in on their secret: they are all

Essex Alumni, Honorary PhDs,
And retired academics: here they live
Forever, but because they have left the

University,
                    they are forever
Deprived   of their departments.

Without hope, they live on in desire.
There's a joke going round campus which sums
Up their plight: "Academics never retire,

They just lose their faculties."'
'My God,' I said, 'you mean they're stuck here
Forever in Limbo? Are there none that

Manage to get away from here?'
'Not many,' he said, 'but occasionally,
When the VC raises the retirement age,

Say, you hear of a lucky few
Who find re-employment in one of our
Partner Colleges: Colchester Institute,

University Campus Suffolk, Writtle College.'
We didn't stop to dawdle while we spoke
But made our way onwards, past a wood.

We had not gone far from where I woke
When I made out a fire burning up ahead,
Which lit up a hemisphere in the darkness.

We were still some distance from it,
But we were close enough for me to begin
To make out some of the shades up there.

'Berrigan,' I said, 'who are these souls
Who seem to occupy some place of special
Honour, set apart from the rest?'

And Berrigan, my guide: 'Their honoured
Names, which still resound in the world of
The living, gain them favour here.

They are poets who once taught here,
Or studied, rare souls,
                        who had the gift of sabi.'

And as he talked I heard a voice exclaim:
'Honour the poet of the New York School!
His shade returns that was departed!'

As the voice fell silent, I saw eight
Shades step towards us, with an aspect
Neither sad nor joyful.

The good master began: 'Mark him
With the Havana cigar clenched in his teeth,
Who walks steadily at the head of the pack,

That's Robert Lowell, the illustrious poet,
Who was once a professor here, in the
70s; the next, just behind him, is

The satirist, Ed Dorn; then look, that stately
Figure with the handlebar moustache is
Tom Raworth, who wrote his *Logbook*

When he was here, but of course, you've met *them*;
Next is Doug Oliver, who descended into
The caves at Winnats Pass to write his epic;

Behind him there's Elaine Feinstein,
Jeremy Reed, who was a student here,
Tony Lopez and Kelvin Corcoran.'

As we drew level with them, they came
To greet Berrigan, and after they had
Talked a while, they turned towards me,

Welcoming me with a gesture, and when
I turned to gaze at Berrigan I saw him smile.
We walked together,

Talking of this and that, until we reached
The boundary of a splendid villa,
Set in a sweet vale all by itself.

It was circled by a security fence,
Bounded by woodland and a clear lake,
And once we had passed through seven

Surveillance gates, like those at Stansted,
We stepped onto a brightly lit lawn.
On it were shades with eyes slow

And grave; they were of great authority
In their demeanour, speaking slowly,
With mild voices. Then moving to one side

In unison, to where the cocktails were
Being handed out, we stepped onto a
Raised veranda, from where they could all be seen.

From this vantage point, as he lit a cigarette,
Berrigan pointed out the illustrious
Shades who peopled the verdant pasture.

There was Charles Leatherland, standing with a group,
Amongst whom was Óscar Arias, the
Nobel Prize Winner, and Dimitrij Rupel,

Foreign Minister of Slovenia.
I saw too Virginia Bottomley,
John Bercow and Siobhain McDonagh,

And when I looked up a little I saw
The master of thought, Simon Critchley,
Chatting away with his philosophical crowd,

Who were hanging on his every word;
I spotted, too, Richard Bartle and Roy
Trubshaw, co-creators of the Multi-User

Dungeon, MUD1, and Rodolfo Vela,
Mexico's first astronaut; then, cracking jokes,
In a way that made them stand out from the crowd,

I saw Nick Broomfield and Mike Leigh, Stephen
Daldry, Lucy Ellmann and Ben Okri,
Who won the Booker Prize.

I can't paint them all in full, as they deserve,
My theme is long, and many times the words
Must fall short of the reality.

The company of ten diminishes to two.
Berrigan leads me by another path,
Out of the quiet, into the trembling air.

I come to a part where there is no light.

CANTO V

We left the garden behind us, descending
By a long track, till we reached Square 2,
Which encompasses less space,

But greater pain. Nearby Todd Landman,
Professor of Government, has his desk,
Where he sits, interrogating new arrivals.

Barely have they entered his room
Than he shows them how many books he's written;
If they have a weakness, he pounces on it,

And he, who is an expert judge,
Then leaps up, winding his scarf round his neck,
And tells them where to go.

'Hi,' he said, when he caught sight of me,
'And welcome to the place where pain is host –
As we say round here, no pain no gain

(That's one from our team in marketing).
Now, please, be careful where you go,
There's a health and safety talk in half an hour,

And an address from our Faculty Manager
Will follow – be warned, it may be easy
To get in, but don't let that deceive you.'

'Put a sock in it you windbag,'
Said Berrigan, 'this one doesn't need
All that bullshit, he's just visiting;

It is willed there where the power is,
That's all
                    you have to know.'

And now the cries of anguish
                    struck my ears
Drowning out all else.

I came to a place void of light
Which rioted like the sea in a tempest
When it is buffeted by warring winds.

The hellish storm
              forever tossed
                    helpless screaming spirits

        into the black air
It was like some infernal
                    fairground ride

And when the faces whirled past our eyes
        they had the look
              of those grown sick with fear.

I learned that to such torment are doomed
The lustful,
                who subject reason to appetite.

As the wings of crows roosting in winter
Bear them along in vast swirling flocks,
        as Mark Cocker has written,

So that blast transported these souls,
Stretching as far as the eye can see.
And I asked: 'Berrigan, tell me,

Who are these people, lashed in the black air?'
'The one who's just going by,'
Berrigan replied, 'is Maeve, Queen of Connacht,

She had so many lovers you couldn't count them,
And more husbands than the Wife of Bath;
In her kingdom she made lust and law alike.

It was she who started the cattle raid
To steal Ulster's prize bull from her former husband,
And there are those who say she had bull-longing.

That other one is Marilyn, who slew
Herself for love, behind her's Berlusconi
Whose scandal knew no shame,

That's King Edward and Mrs Simpson, whose affair
Rocked the crown, then Bill Clinton,
Richard Burton and Elizabeth Taylor,

And there's Paris Hilton…' – then over a thousand
Shades he showed to me, and pointing with
His finger gave me their stories.

When I had heard my teacher name so many,
I was overcome by pity, and felt faint.
'Poet,' I began, 'I would like to talk to

That pair that go together
And seem so light upon the wind.'
'Wait till they're a bit nearer,' he said,

'If you entreat them in the name of
That love they share, they'll come.'
As soon as the wind gusted them towards us

I raised my voice: 'Oh wearied spirits!
Come and speak with us if it isn't forbidden!'
And then, just as on *Shooting Stars*

The dove comes down, when bidden, so those
Spirits issued from the band where Ulrika is,
Such was the power of my call.

When they came into view, I beheld
An aged tutor, balding on top,
And a young student, with coal black hair.

'Oh living creature, gracious and kind,
Who goes through the black air
        to visit us,' said the girl,

'Whatever you wish to hear
        you shall hear it, whilst the wind,
        as now, is silent for us.

The place I was born was Londonderry,
I came here to study,
        and to escape the Troubles.

Love, quick to kindle in a seasoned heart,
Led my tutor to fall for my young body,
And I in turn loved back.'

'Dear creature,' I said, 'the terrible torment
You suffer brings tears of pity
To my eyes,

                but tell me,
How, and by what signs, did love let you
             know your desires?'

And she replied: 'There is no greater pain
Than to recall a happy time from a state
Of wretchedness (as your companion knows)

But if you wish to know
             the first root of our love
             I will tell it, though I weep.

It was the Essex way, when Donald Davie still
Held sway, to teach in tutorials, one on one;
One day, the course was LT361:

Arthurian Literature, we were comparing
Malory with an Old French version of
The legend; we read of Lancelot,

Of how he fell in love, time and again
Our eyes were united by the text,
Gregory tried to impress me with an

Interpretative aside; we blushed.
To the movement of one line alone we yielded:
When we read about the forbidden kiss

Then my teacher kissed me on the mouth
Tremblingly; that book was our Galeotto;
That day we read it no further.'

Whilst the one spirit thus spake she wept
Constantly, while the other bowed his head.
The sight of these wretched souls filled me with pity,

And I fell, as a body, dead, falls.

CANTO VI

Regaining now my senses, which had zoned out
At the sight of that old roué
                         and his student

New wretchedness and new sinners retching
I see, wherever I move,
                         wherever I look.

I am in the sewer that is Square 3,
Fast food joints all around me,
Knee-deep in chip cartons and half-chewed kebabs;

Men in boiler suits hose it with jet sprays,
The dirty water fills the air, like Irish mist,
The stink never leaves the place.

There's a stoner wearing dreads   and
A filthy poncho, with a three-headed
         bulldog on a frayed bit of string,

The dog's six eyes are bloodshot, the three mouths
Black, the three bellies swollen, ribs poking out –
It's like something out of *Harry Potter*.

Spilling from Food on 3 and the SU bar,
Hung-over students howl like mutts
         slipping and sliding   in the filth.

When the slimy hound got a sniff of us,
He pulled on the leash, snarling,
                         showing his fangs.

Berrigan, my guide, bent down slowly,
Without taking his eyes off the beast, and,
     spreading wide   his wiry fingers,

Shovelled up a fistful of spewed-up sausage
And beans, flinging it down those
                         gawping gullets.

As a famished hound, hungering to
Be fed, quiets down when you bring out the Bonzo,
So the filthy heads now ceased their barking.

We walked across this slippery square
Of shades squirming in the soup,
When one of them sat up suddenly:

'You there, on a tour of Hell's diners,'
He beckoned, 'do you not remember my face,
For you were born before I expired.'

I said: 'It may be the torments you
      suffer have disfigured you,
            I can't put a name to your face,

But my memory   is not
What it was
              tell me who you are.'

'Your own city,' he said, 'so full of hate
It overflows the pan,
Once held me in the fresh air above.

Your people called me Round Nick
And I'm damned
             for always stuffing my fat face,

All the bodies flattened here
Share in my sin
             and in my pain.'

'Nick,' I said to him, 'I recall you now,
And your sad suffering makes me weep,
But tell me what'll happen, if you can,

To the people of that   divided state,
And are there any honest men among them?
And tell me, why is it so fucked up?'

'Some blame the Act of Union, some Kitty O'Shea,
Some the Brits, some the Prods, some the IRA,
          but sheer bigotry has played its

Part, coupled with sectarianism
And lust for power. Who knows
   when the violence will run its course?

There are honest men, but no-one wants to know,
For pride and hate and envy are the three
Tunes the Orangemen sing,

They kindle in men's hearts, and set them ablaze.'
With this his dirge ended, but I answered:
'Tell me more, what of

Rowlands, and Trimble, who had such good
Intentions, Cathal Goulding,
Michael Farrell, and the rest,

Bent on doing good? Where are they?
Do they taste Heaven's sweetness
   or Hell's tandoori?'

'Some taste Heaven's sweetness, others lie
Below with blacker souls. If you keep on,
You may see them still. I speak no more.'

He twisted his great head towards me
And eyed me a moment,
Then rolled beneath the scum.

Berrigan, my guide, then spoke:
'He'll wake no more till Donald Davie
Blows his shrill whistle,

Then the dead souls will put on
Flesh once more,
   and face their *viva voce*.'

And so we splashed through the filth
Of goners and doners,
Talking a little of the afterlife.

I said: 'Master, will these torments be increased,
Or lessened, on Finals' Day,
Or will the misery remain the same?'

And Berrigan: 'Remember your theory;
The more a thing is subject to deconstruction,
As Derrida says, the more monstrous

Its pleasure, or its pain.' We
Talked of Foucault, and punishment,
And Ginsters, till we came to a steep bank;

There we found Mervyn King, man's arch-enemy.

CANTO VII

'Give Col a bonus! Give Col a bonus!'
The voice of Mervyn King spat out these words,
And Berrigan, my guide,

Whispered: 'Don't let him freak
You out, he's a powerful mother,
But he can't stop our campus tour.'

Then he turned towards that bloated countenance,
Saying, 'Shut it, moneybags,
Feed on last night's oysters that rot your guts,

This tour of your wretched kingdom
Has Dean's approval, and funding
                    from the AHRC.'

As sails, swollen by wind, collapse
                    when the yacht's mast snaps,
So the savage beast collapsed before our eyes,

And then we started up those slippery steps,
Past wasted students stopped for a smoke,
                    that led to Square 4.

Who could imagine misery
                    as strange as I saw here,
Like something out of   Dalí.

As a speeding car on the road loses its
Grip on the tarmac, spinning into a stream of
Oncoming traffic, so these folk danced the conga;

More sinners were here than anywhere below
And from both sides, to the piercing cry of their
Screams, chests stuck out, they rolled giant coins,

And when they clashed against each other they
Turned to push the other way, one bunch yelling
'What's the point in saving?', the other bunch

'Take out an ISA!' And so they whirled round
A grooved circle of pale concrete, like a
Treadmill, some retreating as far as Barclays,

Some sheltering near the Abbey. Then once more
They clash and turn and roll in their circular joust.
And I, shaken by such a sight,

Turned to Berrigan, my guide: 'Tell me, master,
Who are these wretched souls?
                    Were they all moneylenders?'

He said: 'Up above, the souls
                    you see here
              had such myopic minds

They could not judge with moderation
                    when it came to money. The ones
          with nothing on top were loan-sharks,

Or managed Building Societies, amassing fortunes,
While whole generations went to the wall
                    struggling to pay back mortgages.'

'Ted,' I said, 'if I may, I reckon
I should be able to recognise a few of these,
Not least the shit who sold me shares in Gartmore,

Just before the Credit Crunch.'
And he replied: 'Dream on, buddy,
The undistinguished life

                    of these moneygrubbers
That made them slaves to cash,
Now makes it hard to tell them apart.

Squandering and hoarding robbed them
Of any life, enlisting them in this scrum,
What more can I say?

Here you see the short-lived mockery
Of Capital,
          for which men bicker and connive.

As Dylan said: "All the money
                    you made
                            will never buy back your soul."'

'This Capital you speak of,
              what is it,
                    that has the world so in its clutches?'

And he replied: 'People are mugs,
              things of real value,
                            friendship, love,

Poetry, health,
              they ride over roughshod
                            for a slice of Capital's cake.

Commodity fetishism rules the day
              drowning us in a sea of white goods
                            and smart gadgets,

Online markets transfer empty futures
                    through time and space
                            beyond all human wit to tell.

One state grows fat with power,
                    another lean,
                            according to Capital's law

Which (like a snake in the grass) cannot
                    be seen.
Nothing human can touch it,

Capital divides
                            and rules   its kingdom
Like a greedy spoilt dictator.

Its changing changes never rest,
Now in houses, now in arms, gold, wheat,
Beef, rice, diamonds, manganese,

Tumbling markets keep it constantly
              in motion, as investors come and go,
                            glad to be part of the ride.

But now let us go on to greater sorrow
                night is coming
                        we've no time to lose.'

We crossed Square 4 to the other side,
Past Happy Days, where tomato ketchup spills
Into a trench formed by its overflow;

That stream was darker than blood
And we, accompanied by that shadowy sauce,
Moved down along a strange path.

When it has reached the foot of a
Grey slope, that melancholy stream descends,
                forming a black lake.

And I, peering into its depths,
Could make out muddied students in that slime
Totally naked and their faces mad.

They struck each other not only with hands,
But with their heads and chests and feet,
And tore each other apart with knives.

Berrigan, my guide, said: 'These are the
Souls of Greek and Turkish MA students
Who war on campus after dark,

Full of hate and anger; and beneath
The surface there are arts students
Whose sighs make the bubbles you can see.

Wedged in the slime they say: "We were lazy
Sods and never turned up for lectures;
Most of the time we were completely stoned,

Now we are lazy sods in the black mud."
This is the dirge they gurgle in their throats,
They can't even get their words out properly.'

And so, across the water,
    we circled that disgusting pond
Our eyes glued to the slime swallowers.

We came, at last, to a tower's base.

CANTO VIII

Before we reached the foot
             of that   tower
Our eyes had been glued to its tip

Where two flashlights morsed,
And, so far off our peepers could barely see,
Another flashlight signalled back.

'Don't tell me,' I said, turning to Berrigan,
'We're nicked.' 'No such luck,' he replied,
'Feast your eyes on the filthy water,

You'll see our welcoming party soon enough,
Unless the marsh's vapours
                          hide   it.'

An SLR never shot a bullet
That cut through flesh faster
Than the coracle, covered in Tesco's bags,

That skimmed towards us, drawn by the shades
Of Brent geese, culled for the royal visit,
With a solitary helmswoman, who was yelling:

'Now I've got you, you wretched soul!
Prepare to burn!' 'Hold your geese,
Boudicca,' my guide replied,

'This dude's just visiting.' If you've seen
Someone looking real pissed when they find
Out they've been swindled – that was Boudicca.

As Berrigan stepped into the coracle
             he handed me a pill,
                          saying,

'You might need one of these,'
And only when I followed
             did the coracle begin to rock.

As we cruised the course of that dead lake
Before me there rose up a mud-bespattered shape,
Saying: 'Who are you, come before you're called?'

And I replied: 'Though I come here, I've
No intention of staying; but who are you
Sporting that mud-soaked mullet?'

'As you can see,' he said, 'I'm one who weeps.'
'Weep on,' I replied, 'for even covered in that
Stinking slime, I recognise you.'

Like a zombie he reached out to rock the boat,
But Berrigan my guide pushed him off with a kick,
Saying: 'Get down there with the other dogs!'

Then he hugged me,
            saying: 'God bless you!
            Up above this arrogant arsehole

Was obsessed with promotion,
        selling himself to the highest bidder,
            like the Whore of Babylon.

Many in LiFTS think themselves great scholars,
        who here will wallow like pigs in muck,
            leaving behind their repulsive fame.

In life he did nothing good, and so
        his shade is filled with rage.'
'Master,' I said, 'call me a sadist,

But I'd love to see him dumped
                deep in the   slop,
                before we leave.'

'Just watch,' Berrigan replied, and soon after
I saw the wretch set upon
                by a crowd:

'Get Harry Potter!' they all shouted,
And at that war cry the Frankfurter, gone mad,
Turned on himself and bit his own fingers,

The blood oozing like ketchup.
We left him there, I'll say no more about him.
The sound of drum and bass began to pound my ears

And made me peer ahead across the water.
'Approaching,' said Berrigan, 'is Cannabis Castle,
with its iron walls and its hardened dopers.'

And I: 'Already I can see the
        bright glow of the spliffs
                        across the swamp.'

And he to me: 'Those are rather fires,
From nightlights carelessly left burning
On stereos and televisions,

Causing the eternal conflagration
                that burns within,
        that no fire-extinguisher can put out.'

We sailed around till at last we
        reached the shore, where Boudicca shouted:
'Alight here! This is the entrance-way!'

I saw the best minds of the Student Union
Perched above the gates, enraged, screaming:
'Who's this cunt approaching? Who, without a

Student card, dares to enter the kingdom of
The dead?' My wise teacher flashed his ID,
Asking to speak to them in private.

They suppressed their rage enough to say:
'You may enter, but that breather
                        goes no further.

Let him retrace his fool's path
                alone, let's see him try.
You're staying right here where you belong!'

Gentle reader, imagine how I shat myself,
When those words reached my ears!
I thought I'd never see the light of day more.

'Ted,
      don't leave me here,
                        I beg you!' I cried,

'If we can't go any further,
      let's turn tail now,
                  while we still can.'

Then Berrigan, who had guided me this far,
Took out his Lucky Strikes,
            and offered me a smoke.

'Wait here,' he said, 'and don't despair yet.
You can bet your bottom dollar
            I won't leave you in this hell-hole.'

At this, he walked away,
            to parley with them,
Leaving me to battle with my thoughts.

I couldn't hear what he proposed,
      but they were having none of it.
I saw them turn

            and shut the heavy gates
In Berrigan's face.
            He turned towards me

His eyes downcast,
      playing with his beard.
'Who are these shits to forbid my entrance

To the halls of grief?
            But don't worry,
They haven't got a leg to stand on.

This insolence of theirs is nothing new,
They showed it once before, at the Knowledge Gateway,
Which I can assure you

            is now unlocked.
You saw the deadly words inscribed on its portals.
And now, already through them, comes one

Who will open this fucking gate for us.'

CANTO IX

When I saw Berrigan bounced back,
Anger painting his complexion red,
I turned white as a sheet;

He tried to calm himself,
Taking a long drag
                    on his cigarette.

'Why the Hell are they blocking our path,
Surely... but no, we've been promised help
From the highest authority,

We just need to play it cool.'
I saw all too clearly how his words
Plastered over a niggling doubt,

And couldn't help imagining the worst:
This is where our journey ends,
And there's no way back.

Tentatively, I put the question to him:
'Has anyone from your circle
Ever entered the halls before?'

At first he looked at me frowningly,
Then he chuckled,
                    flicking away his ash.

'I see where you're coming from,' he said.
'Only once in a blue moon
                    is someone foolish enough

To make this trip on which I go,
But in fact I've been down here
                    once before.

We were running out of weed,
Not to mention amphetamines,
And Ed Dorn bet me a quarter

I couldn't blag my way in here to score.
Security wasn't so tight back then,
I followed the beat up to the tenth floor

Where a guy called Rots used to have digs,
A maths student who supported himself by dealing.
To cut a long story short, I won the bet.'

He said more, too, but I forget the details,
For suddenly my eyes were drawn upwards
To a window near the top of the tower

Where three drunk students
Were leaning out, their hair dyed blonde,
Their look betraying a bad attitude.

They had fuck-off faces, heavily beslapped,
Their eyebrows studded with diamonds,
And round their bare waists hung gold chains.

Berrigan, who knew well the SU crowd,
Cried out:
                    'Look! The Essex Girls!

That's Big Meg, the one on the left,
And that one raving on the right's Sexy Lexi,
Tiffany's the one in the middle.'

In a flash they stuck out their tits
Then turned round
                            to show us their arses.

'Jordan, over 'ere, we'll give him a boner!'
They shouted, leering down at us
Through false eyelashes.

'Turn around now and shut your eyes,'
Said my gentle guide, 'for if Jordan comes,
No mortal can resist her charms.'

Thus spoke Berrigan, who stubbed out his fag,
And turned me around himself,
Putting his sticky fingers over my eyes.

(All of you here who understand textual
Analysis and hermeneutics, note
The symbolism in the above passage;

Any resemblance of the characters
To persons living or dead
Is coincidental.)

And then, across the filthy water,
Came an explosion of sound
Which made both sides of the lake tremble.

It sounded like one of those freak hurricanes
Whipped up by the clash of counter-temperatures
That tear through buildings and streets

Tossing trees and cars aloft like toys.
Berrigan freed my eyes and said:
'Now turn round and take a look across

The pond, there where the mist is thickest.'
And as my eyes once more adjusted to
The light, I saw the figures

In the mud swim for all they were worth,
As frogs will flee a lawnmower,
To get out of the way of a jet-ski

Which tore across the swelling waters
Scything off ears and toes as it went
Carrying a man who must be the head porter.

I turned round to speak to Ted
But he made me a secret sign
Telling me straight away to zip the lip

In the presence of this man from security.
Oh, what scorn poured forth from his lips,
Aimed at the surly students,

As he reached the heavy gates
To the burning tower, pulled out his keys,
And opened them without resistance.

'You bunch of utter wankers!
How dare you piss about like this
And get me out at this time of the night.

Any more trouble like this
And the lot of you will face disciplinary action.
And turn that fucking noise down while you're at it!'

He turned round then and rode back,
Across the squalid swan's road,
Answering a call on his mobile,

And on his furrowed brow you could see
The look of one with different worries
That were not those he found surrounding him.

We entered the tower without opposition,
And I, anxious to investigate the
Students who lodged in such a fortress,

                cast my eyes about,
And saw in every direction
A dwelling of desolation and abjection.

As at Arles, where the Rhone stagnates,
Or as at St Mary's in Colchester,
Where the lids of the sepulchres

Are broken
                and cast about,
So the rooms here were in a mess,

And burning all about were fierce flames
Which kept the rooms far hotter
Than any summer barbecue.

Each room had its fire-door loose, torn off
                at the hinges,
And from within came fierce laments.

'Master,' I asked, 'what souls are these who,
Stuck in these stinking digs,
Make themselves known by their powerful sighs?'

And Berrigan replied: 'Here lie wasters,
Addicts, gluttons and party-goers,
A lazy bunch who rarely leave their rooms

Except to get a fix or pick a fight.
All sorts are crammed in here,
Left to cook like baked potatoes.'

Then, after turning at the top of the stairs,
We passed a kitchen
                    bellowing acrid smoke,

And continued our ascent.

CANTO X

Now by a narrow stairwell
Between the lift-shaft and the outer wall
My master went on, and I behind.

'Dear Berrigan,' I said, 'trusted guide,
Who leads me through these smoking squats,
Tell me, will we get a chance to see

The souls who lie within these rooms?
The doors are off,
          and nobody's standing guard.'

To which Berrigan: 'You should bear in mind
The lesson which helped you get out of
Belfast alive: "Let sleeping dogs lie."'

At Berrigan's words, a man wearing
The bloodied apron of a butcher,
Who at first I mistook for a student

In fancy dress, poked his reddened
Face out of a smoking doorway,
And eyed us up and down with a look of

Astonishment. 'What are you doing here,'
He said, 'a living soul patrolling the corridors
Of the dead? And did I hear you mention

Belfast, that strife-torn city, which once
I called home?' With a gentle push
Berrigan encouraged me to move forwards

Towards the door: 'Choose your words with care,'
He whispered. 'Tell me,' I said,
'For I too hail from that self-same city,

Though my accent has faded with time,
Forced into exile as I was
Still in the flush of youth,

What part did you play in the troubled
Past of that bloody city?' At that
He pulled himself up with pride

Smoothing his apron down with his hands,
And spoke: 'Young man, let me tell you,
I ran a salutary business in the

Pork trade, and I pride myself to this day
That it was my pork sausages,
Not an inferior variety, like those

Supplied by Walls or Colin Glenn,
That fed the paras and the RUC,
Not to mention the students of this establishment,

Till the dirty Fenians took revenge,
Burning down all my slaughterhouses
Till in the end I was almost glad of the day

They showed up at my door dressed in
Balaclavas, carrying their sawn-off shotguns
Like the cowards they were, and blew my face off.'

By the time he had finished speaking
I had reached the threshold of his room.
He looked me in the eye and asked,

Half-contemptuously: 'And who would your ancestors be?'
And I, who wanted only to oblige him,
Held nothing back, but told him freely

All he might wish to know. At which
He raised his brows a little, then said:
'Your family, then, must have been the owners of

That damned dog that roamed
The streets like a vagabond, and never let off
Pestering my bitches when they were in heat.

Not once, but twice, I dragged him back
To your house by the scruff of his neck,
Swearing if he ever showed his face again

I'd make him into sausage meat!'
Just then, round the same door's battered frame,
A shadow arose, visible to the chin;

It raised itself upon its knees
And looked about as if it hoped to see
Whether someone else was accompanying me,

And when its expectation was quenched
It stuttered, weeping: 'If it be genius
That gives you the right to freely roam

This blind prison, where is my boy,
Whose scholarship in US Studies
Is second to none, and why

Is he not by your side?' 'I'm not alone,'
I said, 'that man who waits over there
Guides me through this stinking cauldron,

A poet, perhaps, your Owen held in scorn?'
(His face, and the question he posed, revealed his name
To me, and made my pointed answer possible.)

At once, he sprang up to his full height and cried:
'What did you say? He *held?* Is he not living then?'
And when he heard the silence

                         of my delay
In responding to his question, he fell back
Into his room, not to be seen again.

The other shade, who'd been talking before,
Showed no concern at all, but turned to me,
Picking up where he'd left off:

'Tell me, for you might know the answer,
Why did Essex cancel its contracts with me
In the 1970s? What was wrong with my bangers?'

'I'm sure there was nothing wrong with them,"
I said, 'but the students of that day
Were mostly hippies, vegetarians who stuck

Two fingers up at the meat industry;
They were the generation that picketed
The livestock exports from Brightlingsea:

Butchery was out of fashion.' 'Unjust! Unjust!'
He cried, 'A bunch of pot-smoking good-for-nothings!
Let me tell you now, for the record,

This craze for vegetarianism, of which you speak,
Is one whose years are numbered;
Before the passage of fifty moons

It will have died out completely;
And in days to come the fur trade too
Will make a healthy comeback:

Not far off lies the day when coats
Of mink and fox fur, badger, bear,
And even Dalmatian will again be worn with pride!'

'I'll believe it when I see it,' I said,
'But tell me, can you answer a question
That's been bugging me:

If I understand correctly, all of you
Can see ahead to what the future holds,
But your knowledge of the present is shaky.'

'Here we see like those with an eye defect,'
He said, 'what's in the distance we see
Clearly, with 20/20 vision,

But when an object is up close
It's all a blur; without gossip
We'd know nothing of your living state.'

Then, moved by regret for what I'd done
I said: 'Will you tell your room-mate
His son is still among the living,

And if, when he asked, I held my silence,
Let him know that as he spoke all my thought
Was taken up with that point you've explained.'

Berrigan had begun to call me back,
So quickly I asked the shade to tell me
What other souls were cooking in this tower.

He said: 'More than a thousand souls lie here
With me, among them some of the Angry Brigade,
One of them's another poet

Wrongly imprisoned in life,
Who now spends her days imprisoned here,
Anna Mendelssohn, also known as Grace,

Of the rest I speak not.' Then he was gone,
And I turned back towards Berrigan,
Thinking on what this man had said about the fur trade.

We moved on, and as we went, Berrigan asked:
'What's bugging you now? You look like you've seen a ghost!'
And I satisfied him in his question.

'Look,' he said firmly, 'what these people say needs
To be taken with a pinch of salt.'
Then he turned to the left, up a stairway,

And we were nearly knocked out by a fearful stink.

CANTO XI

'That smell,' said Berrigan, 'comes from the bins
Which lie below, full of uneaten food and
Stinking rubbish – the bad news is that

It gets worse the closer you get to it,
And we're heading that way.' Before I had
A chance to protest, Berrigan had summoned

The lift which took us down in seconds,
Then we proceeded a little way on foot.
The place we came to was the edge of a steep bank

Composed of broken concrete, mud and steel,
And here the stench was so powerful
We had to step back from the precipice.

Not far from where we stood, Berrigan
Drew my attention to a giant skip
Awaiting collection. On stepping closer,

I saw it was labelled DISSERTATIONS.
Berrigan noticed the look of shock on my face,
And tried to reassure me: 'Not all

Dissertations suffer this ignoble fate,'
He said, 'these are the ones that didn't toe the
Line, students who used Freud with Jungians,

Others who used Derrida with Lacanians.
The rest are stored in the library.
Until our noses get used to the stink

We'd better shelter behind this skip,
Once we've been here a bit you'll hardly notice it.'
'Is there something we can do to pass the time?'

I asked. 'Don't worry,' said Berrigan, 'I've
Thought of that.' He began to roll a huge joint,
And as he did so, he said: 'Beneath these rocks

Lie many more souls packed in; and since later
The sight of them will be enough, I'll tell you a
Little about them.' 'While you're at it,' I added,

'Could you also explain the layout of the campus?
At times I find it hard to fathom.'
'That's a tough ask,' he said, 'but I'll do my best.

Putting it simply, things used to be arranged
Round the five squares and the points of the compass,
But as the campus expanded, this system

Became rapidly obsolete. Besides, it was
Never very helpful –
Students could rarely find their way to class.

In fact, there's a rumour that a student
From the 1960s is still walking about somewhere,
Looking for the Lecture Theatre Block.

The new layout (which in reality
Coexists alongside the old one,
Like the imperial and metric systems)

Is simpler: the campus is divided into Zones,
1–9, and each Zone into Areas, A–Z.
This system has the advantage of allowing

For almost infinite expansion,
And it's useful in case of fire drills and the like,
Which round here are pretty common, as you can imagine.'

Berrigan stopped for a moment, to lick the joint,
And I took the opportunity to ask
About the souls who were confined below.

'OK,' he said, 'Martin Luther King put it well
When he said, "Those who assert that evil means
Can lead to good ends are deceiving themselves."

All malice has injustice as its end,
And this is achieved by violence or by fraud;
As fraud belongs exclusively to humanity

It is all the more despicable.
In the first Zone below, Zone 7,
You'll find the violent, but since there are different

Kinds of violence, it's divided into
Three Areas: 7A contains
Homicides, 7B suicides and

Squanderers, 7C the blasphemers
And usurers, amongst others.
Beyond that, in Zones 8 and 9, as you'll

See, things get worse: down there you'll find all
Sorts of fraud of the worst kind: hypocrites,
Of which there's no shortage amongst academics,

Those who waste their time making crazy predictions,
Cheats and thieves, moneygrubbers, grafters
And like filth.' 'Master,' I said, 'I'm beginning

To get the picture, but tell me, what about
The souls we passed earlier on, those
Swept by the winds and lashed by the hoses,

Those stuck in the muddy swamp, why aren't they
Too shut inside the burning gates?'
'Didn't they teach you anything at that

Grammar school of yours? You mean you haven't
Read the *Nicomachean Ethics*? Where do I
Begin? Aristotle distinguishes between

Three kinds of wrong: to put it crudely,
He calls them incontinence, malice, and
Bestiality. Incontinence, he argues,

Is the least of the three evils, and if
You think back to the kind of shades we met
Early on in our journey, you'll see why they

Suffer less. Are you with me?' 'I was never
Too hot at classics,' I said, 'I once got
2% in a Latin exam, but I get your drift.

Tell me, though, what's the problem with usury?
Surely we need people to lend us money,
Otherwise how would you buy a house, for example?'

'Mortgages,' said Berrigan, 'are a con,
It's just another form of robbery.
This was one thing old Ez got right,

Even if he got it wrong about the Jews
And the fascists – read canto XLV
Where he puts it plainly:

"with usura, sin against nature,
is thy bread ever more of stale rags
is thy bread dry as paper,

with no mountain wheat, no strong flour
with usura the line grows thick
with usura is no clear demarcation

and no man can find site for his dwelling.
Stone cutter is kept from his stone
weaver is kept from his loom…"

Now, speaking of stone, it's about time
We picked ourselves up again, and had
A closer look at this landfall,

We need to think about making our way down.'

CANTO XII

The point we came to, to make our
Descent, not far from Reception,
            was steep and treacherous.

As, at Aberfan, when
      the mountainous slag heap
Collapsed

         burying the town,
Slurry, mud and concrete
           littered our track,

And guarding the way was that monstrous
Bigot, John Bull, in his
            top hat and braces,

A bunch of skinheads
        with Nazi tats
      at his side.

When he saw us approaching
He tucked his thumbs behind his braces,
        whispering something to his friends.

Berrigan, my guide, lit the spliff,
      and as we drew near,
           he held it out to the skins.

'Fancy a smoke, boys?' he asked,
And at once one of their number
          reached out a hand to snatch it.

They sat down amongst the rocks to smoke,
As John Bull stood there, fuming with rage.
'Quick,' my shrewd guide called out, 'let's go,

Before things turn nasty.' And so we went down,
      over the scree
         which I felt shift and tilt

Beneath my feet
          with the human weight
                    it was not used to.

I was in deep thought when Berrigan began:
'Are you wondering what made the podium
          collapse, making this heap of rubble,

Down which we clamber? Last time
          I was here, as visiting professor,
                    it still stood firm.

Yet, if I remember well, that was just before
The helicopter, carrying scouts from Vanderbilt, came,
          to cream off any talent they could find,

Then this abyss of stench began to quake,
From top to bottom, that was the moment the
Concrete began to split – here, and in other places.

But now, look out across the marshes,
Towards B&Q, coming closer you will see
          the river of blood that boils the souls

Of those who injured others through violence.'
          I saw a river – wide, bent like the pin of
                    a grenade – embracing the bleak flatlands,

Across which came an
          army of cleaners, trotting in single file,
                    armed with mops and buckets.

Catching sight of us, they stopped short
And three of them approached: 'You there,
On your way to the river like a couple of rats,

What torture are you looking for? Speak,
Or I'll give you a taste of my mop.'
                    And then Berrigan called back:

'We'll give our answer to Sharon, when we're
At her side; as for you, I see you're
                    surly as ever!'

He nudged me, whispering: 'That one there is
Trevor, a right bastard, who went down for
GBH before he landed a job here.

The middle one, with the tits,
            is Sharon   an ex-student, who did a
                    PhD on Achilles and homoeroticism.

The last is Jock, an ex-para who
Fired the first shot on Bloody Sunday,
                        known for his short temper.'

When we got closer to the bunch,
            Sharon took out her vanity case,
And began to   powder her nose,

Then she opened her cavernous mouth and spoke
To Trev and Jock: 'Have you noticed how
The one behind moves what he touches?

This is not what dead men's feet would do.'
And Berrigan replied: 'You're right,
                            he is no dead man,

He travels along this dismal estuary
                        by necessity, not pleasure,
To see how the dead live.

Now, give us a guide for God's sake,
One who knows the area,
To lead us safely along the river,

I want to show this one the souls
Who suffer.' Sharon looked over her
                right breast and said to Trevor:

'You go, Trev, guide them as they ask, and
If the boss grumbles, I'll tell him where to go.'
And so we moved off, along the stinking

River's bank, where piercing shrieks rose
From the boiling sewer. There I saw
People sunk   to their eyelids,

As the surly cleaner explained:
'These are tyrants who dealt in blood,
With hot tears they pay for their crimes.

Here stand Sidney and the unmoveable Trevelyan,
Who weighed down Ireland with years of pain,
And there, that forehead smeared with coal-black hair,

Is Bernadette Devlin; the other one,
The blonde, is Myra Hindley.'
I looked up at Berrigan, but he said:

'Let him instruct you now, don't look to me.'
            A little farther on, the cleaner stopped
               above some souls peering from the blood,

Which here reached to their throats.
He pointed out a shade off to one side,
Alone   and said:

'That one, if I'm not mistaken, is Sam Cooke,
Who took a Catholic girl back to his room
To strangle her, cutting her

Throat before he dumped the body   on
Waste ground.' Then I saw other souls,
Their heads and chests above the blood,

And I knew the faces of many who were there.
Then the river's blood began decreasing, till
It cooked the toes and nothing more,

And here was a signed footpath, which we could follow
At ease. 'Just as the river gets shallower on this
Side,' said the surly cleaner,

'On the other side it gets deeper,
Till it reaches the spot where tyrants moan.
There you will find Raleigh   and Essex,

And, sunk deepest of all,
                        William of Orange,
Whose battlefields were highways of blood.'

Then he turned back, and retraced his steps.

CANTO XIII

Trevor had not yet reached the bridge by B&Q
When we found ourselves entering a wood
Marked by a narrow dirt track.

The leaves were not green, but black,
Nor were the branches straight
        but gnarled and twisted,

And each tree bore a laminated white label,
Grown illegible through wear,
And wilted flowers at the base of the trunk.

No holts so rough or dense have those wild fowl,
That flee all cultivated tracts,
Between Mersea Island and Maldon.

Here the Essex Harpies twine their nests,
Whose namesakes chased the Trojans
From the Strophades, with prophecies of doom,

A mutant breed, sired at Bradwell,
Where the reactor leaks its waste
Into the Blackwater.

Wide wings they have, necks and faces of women,
Their feet are clawed like the falcon,
Their fat bellies feathered.

Raising his voice to drown out their piercing shrieks
Berrigan said: 'Look closely about you
And you will see with your own eyes

What I won't waste time describing, for if I did,
You wouldn't credit it.' Already I heard wailing
From every side, but could see nobody there.

I reckon Berrigan thought I was imagining
That the voices echoing around those stumps
Came from people who hid themselves on our account,

For he said: 'Reach out, and break off
A branch from one of these trees,
Then what you're thinking now will break off too.'

I stretched my hand a little into the air
And snapped off a branch from a thorn tree;
The trunk cried out: 'What the fuck?'

And when the wound had grown dark with blood
It again began to cry: 'Why are you roughing me up?
What the fuck have I done to you?

If I was still a man, I'd take you both on,
But even if I was the soul of a shit,
You could show me a wee bit of respect.

We were students once, now we are turned to wood,
Not because we were thick, mind you,
Now show a little pity, for Christ's sake!'

As a green log, burning at one end,
Hisses and oozes sap from the other,
So from that splintered trunk

Words and blood poured forth at once;
I let the branch drop from my fingers
And stood as one petrified by fear.

'Lighten up,' said Berrigan, 'it's only a scratch.
If my companion here had read his Virgil
More carefully, and credited what's written there,

He would not have reached out his hand against you,
But the incredibility of the thing
Made me egg him on.

But tell him who you were; to make up he can
Carry your story back to the world above,
Where his return is sure.'

'Seeing as you're asking,
I was a border at Colchester Grammar,
Known for my attitude

And my way with the women.
I was never happier than at a party,
A drink in one hand and a fag in the other.

Later, my love for the booze
    led me on to harder drugs
        till I ended up on smack,

Drifting into a life of squatting
And petty theft with some old schoolmates.
        Eventually, determined

To turn things round, I came here to study,
But soon fell into debt. I hadnae any choice
But to start dealing to pay it off.

And it wasnae long before the Dean here
Got wind of it, inflaming the hearts of
Everyone against me,

Till my attempt to gain honours turned to tears.
I could brook it no longer, so one day
I just took an overdose, and that was me done.'

Berrigan listened, then said to me:
'Seeing as he's silent now
        ask him if there's more you wish to know.'

'No, please, Ted,' I said, 'you question him.
I can't, pity so chokes me.'
Then Berrigan turned once more towards the shade,

Asking: 'So we might better understand your state,
Tell us how a soul
        gets bound in these knots.'

Then the trunk blew strongly, and soon that wind
Formed into words: 'What you ask is easy
To answer. I shall be brief.

When the angry spirit quits the body
From which it has torn itself,
Todd Landman, Professor of Government,

Judges it, then kicks it out.
It falls into the wood, and wherever it falls,
There it sprouts, like grain of spelt;

There's a brief ceremony, where they give you
A label and a number, and sometimes
A mourner passes with some flowers.

The grain grows into a sapling, then a tree;
At last, the Harpies come, then feeding
On the leaves, give pain, and to pain a way out.'

We stood there all ears, listening to the trunk,
Thinking it would tell us more, when we
Were surprised by a sudden noise,

Like that a hunter hears
As the pack closes in for the kill,
                    beast and branches crashing;

Then to the left of where we stood
        appeared two shapes, part human part fox,
        their faces those of Cameron and Clegg,

Fleeing with such haste
That they tore away with them the branches.
'Let me fess up,' said the first, seeing us standing there,

'I was never in favour of lifting the ban.'
Then to the other, who couldn't keep up, he yelled:
'I've never seen you change direction so quickly

Since you changed your mind over tuition fees!'
And then, through shame, Clegg
Slipped into a bush and hid amongst the thorns.

Behind these pitiful souls, who had squandered power,
The wood was overrun by black bitches,
Fleet as greyhounds on the track at Romford.

Into the one who hid they sank their teeth,
Tearing him apart piece by piece
Then ran off with his miserable limbs.

Berrigan now took me by the hand
And drew me towards the bush
Which was lamenting from every sore.

'Oh Nick Clegg!' it cried, 'See what good
It's done you to take cover in me.
Was it my fault if your policies backfired?'

Then Berrigan spoke to the bush, saying:
'Who were you, who spit your words
                          through so many wounds?'

And he replied: 'You spirits who have
Come in time to see this unjust mutilation
That has torn me from all my leaves,

Sweep them up quick, and restore them
To their owner. I come from that proud
City torn with strife, which made its wealth

In the linen trade and shipbuilding.
I was foreman when they made the
Titanic, that fated ship that struck the iceberg;

That same day, I made my home my gibbet.'

CANTO XIV

Love of my native city moved me to
Gather up the scattered leaves and give them
Back to him whose voice was already growing hoarse.

Then we reached a break
                              in the woodland
And came to a new place of pain.

We looked out over bare flatlands,
Stretching as far as the eye can see,
Where few plants grow,

Only reeds and wormwood,
      so barren   is the earth;
The mournful wood borders them

Like a lonely wreath, and is
Bordered in turn
                              by the river of blood

Which runs beside a wide rim of sand,
Thick and burning, like that packed down
By coalition boots in Iraq.

The place was swarming with herds of souls,
Some who walked naked,
                              like sun-lovers,

Some who were heavily dressed, as if for winter,
All cursing, or muttering incomprehensibly,
Or simply wailing,

So that the air was filled with their eerie music.
Of these, some lay sprawled across the sand,
Some sat crouched in the hollows

Of the marsh, while others roamed incessantly
Up and down, like dog owners
                              who had lost their mutts.

Over the sand, falling slowly,
Rained flakes of burning fire, like those
Of snow that fall in the Alps on a windless day,

Or those that Saddam Hussain saw raining
On his troops as they retreated across Iraq's
Torrid lands, exploding

When they hit the ground, so that his men
And their vehicles
                    burned up as they fled;

Here
        sand and reeds were kindled,
Like tinder under flint and steel,

Redoubling pain. Ever restless was the dance
Of scorched fingers, now here, now there,
Shaking off the fresh burning.

'Berrigan, my guide,' I began, 'you who
Can conquer all things (except those angry students
Who shut the gate on us at the tower)

Who is that great spirit, who seems to care not
For the fire, that lies disdainful and contorted,
As if the rain didn't bother him?'

As I spoke, the man raised himself up unsteadily
On the sand, waving an empty bottle of Bushmills
In our faces, then spoke in a drawl:

'What I was living, I am too dead,
A Fenian, an alcoholic and a junky,
Like James Clarence fucking Mangan,

And a better singer of the songs
You'll not find this side of Lethe's waters!
Up in the light I took my share of the shite:

I've been raped and spat on and shat on and abused,
Kicked in the teeth till the blood came out my ears
By Her Majesty's men in the blue cloth.

There's nothing this side of Hell's gates
I haven't seen before, I tell you;
But would you be having any cheap pills,

If you know what I mean,
Your fellow there looks like a man
After my own taste.'

Then Berrigan spoke back: 'Shane MacGowan,
It's you, isn't it? You haven't lost any
Of your blustering pride, have you?

But you've had a skinful already,
Perhaps that's why you pay no attention
To these searing flakes, I'm not handing out

Any free pills to you.' And then he turned
His face to me, saying: 'That man was once king
Of the hit parade, one of the seven Pogues,

He blasphemed his way to the top of the charts,
Then all the way down again, till he ended
Up in the state you see him in now.

Now follow me, and see you don't step
On the burning sand, but stick
To the straight track close to the wood.'

In silence we came to a spot where a
Thick concrete pipe carried toxic effluent
Off the farmland, spewing it into the

Waters of the river of blood (its stink
Still sticks in my nostrils!). As I gazed out
Across the estuary, a thought framed

Itself in my mind, and wishing to know
The answer I asked Berrigan why it was
That the river flowed red.

'Not far from campus,' said Berrigan,
'There lies a place they call Colchester,
Where the British Army rest

Between tours of duty,
And under whose king, Cymbeline,
              the world once knew peace.

Before that, the Romans built their capital here,
Camulodunum. North of there, the Iceni
Still ruled, a warrior race,

But when their king – I forget his name – died,
The Romans turned on his widow;
She was whipped publicly and her daughters raped.

This was a big mistake: Boudicca
Turned the might of her army on
Camulodunum and torched it.

The Romans, mostly retired veterans,
Took refuge in the Temple of Claudius,
But this didn't do them much good.

Boudicca torched that too, and to this day,
If you dig down, you can still see a seam
Of burnt red clay, the destruction layer.

It's the blood she spilt that makes the river
Colne run red, and it's this river that
Encircles the campus and feeds the lakes,

One of which, as you have seen,
              she still sails
                    in her coracle.'

Then I asked another thing that had been
Puzzling me: 'Where is the river Lethe, then,
Of which MacGowan spoke?'

'Hold your horses,' said Berrigan, 'we've still
Got a long way to go. You'll see your Lethe
In good time, if we get out of this abyss.

That's where the shades go to wash themselves
When their guilt is taken off by penitence.
Now it's time to move on,

See that you follow me, and stick to the raised track.'

CANTO XV

As the Flemings between Wissant and Bruges,
In fear of the flood tides' constant threat,
Build strong dykes to repel the sea;

And as Canvey islanders,
Fearful of another flood like in '53,
Raise up barrages against the estuary,

In like fashion were these banks built,
Though not so high or so large,
By Roman hands, from mud and oyster shells.

We had left the wood behind us,
So far back, indeed, that had I turned
To look I couldn't have seen it,

When we met a troop of spirits
Who walked beside the bank, on the sand;
From where they'd come from, in the distance,

The eye could make out barbecues,
Which lit up the water's edge,
Flinging sparks high into the air;

As they approached, each one peered at us,
As in the evening clubbers
Look at one another under the lamplight,

And as they drew level, one of their number,
Recognising me, grabbed me by the sleeve,
And said: 'Well I never!'

And I, as he stretched out his arm,
Fixed my eyes on his sun-tanned brow,
And bending my face down to look him

In the eye, exclaimed: 'Is this really
You here, Dr Moss?' And he, laughing,
Exclaimed: 'We've been having a barbecue,

A whole crowd of us, it's such a lovely evening.
Shall I join you for a walk, if I'm not
Too drunk to climb up the bank?'

'Be my guest,' I said, lending him a hand.
Once on the bank, we sat down on a bench,
Sharing a cigarette with Berrigan, my guide.

'If you don't mind me asking,' he said,
'What brings you down here at this late hour,
And who's this one showing you the way?'

'This is the poet, Ted Berrigan,' I said,
'I bumped into him by the cash machines,
And he's giving me a tour. How's things?

How's the novel going? *The Book of Carthage*,
Or was it Chiswick?' 'You remember that?'
He said. 'Well, the title's changed several

Times since then, but it's pretty much done.
The market, though, is unforgiving these days.
If I'd finished it a few years back,

When novels about Muslims were still new,
It might have stood a chance – as things are,
I have my doubts.

How are things with you? Still doing poems?
How's Ann? How's the department?'
'Oh, it's OK,' I said, 'You know,

Nothing much changes.' 'Well, don't let them drag
You down,' he said, 'these ungrateful
And malignant scholars will become,

For your good work, your enemies – and not
Without reason: among the bitter berries
Is no fit place for the ripe fig to bloom.

But if you keep writing, things will work out.
Steer a path between the mainstream and the
Experimenters, that way nobody can claim you,

You'll always be your own man.'
'Oh, if everything I wished had been granted,'
I replied, 'they'd have made a chair for you.

My mind is still etched
With your early encouragement of my work,
When I showed you my first primitive efforts,

Playing about with Aesop – in fact I still have
Your copy of L'Estrange somewhere,
And I'm not about to give it back.

Your example first showed me how I might
Combine a job in teaching with the real
Work of writing, and while I live

I'll always talk of my debt to you,
And of my gratitude. I'll remember what
You tell me, and chew it over.'

Berrigan, hearing this, stood up, stubbing
Out his cigarette, then looked at me and said:
'He hears the best who pays the closest heed.'

I didn't answer him, but went on talking
With Dr Moss, asking him
Who of his company I might know of.

'You might have heard of one or two of them,'
He said, 'but I doubt it. About some of
Them, the less said the better.

Many are writers, some academics,
One of them's a priest who works
Not far from me, in Kemptown.

Oh, and Jeff's there, along with his partner –
Have you met that guy? I could go on, but
Time's too short, there's such a crowd.

Look, I'd better be making tracks,
I see another barbecue coming to an end,
And there are some people there I'd rather avoid.

Remember my *Pink Pagoda*,
That's one thing I ask of you, and don't forget
The Secret Life and Mysterious Death of Mr Chinn!'

Then he turned back, and he seemed like
One of those who race for the green cloth
At Verona, through the open fields, and like

The winner of the group, not the last man in.

CANTO XVI

As we made our way along the steep bank,
Bordering the river of blood,
We passed through a second wood, and when we

Emerged, we found ourselves in a place
Where the burning
                        flakes   of flame

Fell   fiercer than ever.
Distant, I could hear the clanking of some
Infernal engine, like the banging that

Car mechanics make, when three shades together,
Running, broke away
                        from a group toasting on the sands.

They veered towards us and, shouting as one, cried:
'You there! Stop!' Then one of them added as
Coda: 'From the look of you, you're from New York –

I'd recognise that face anywhere!'
As they drew closer, what wounds I saw
By the flames burned in –

It pains me yet, as I write these lines.
My teacher listened to their cries, then
Turning towards me, said: 'Hold it;

These guys deserve a little respect.
In fact, if it weren't for those burning flakes
Raining down over the sands, I'd suggest

You ran to greet them, not vice versa.'
We stopped, as they came up to the foot of the bank,
Where they stopped too, forming themselves into

A wheel;
It made me think of Matisse's dancers
Whirling in a ring,

As if they were trying to make of their lives,
Of their deaths,
                    a work of high art.

Spinning around in this way, each one
Flung his head towards us as he whizzed past
So that their necks and feet appeared

To move constantly in opposite directions.
As they continued spinning, one of them began:
'Ted Berrigan, it's been a long time!

If the misery of these sterile sands
And our blotched and scorched demeanour
Doesn't scare you off, talk to us a while;

And you there, who seem to be a living shade,
Walking unpunished through these torrid zones,
Let our fame persuade you to tell us who you are.

He in whose footsteps you see me tread,
All naked and peeling though he is now,
Was of noble station, more than you may know;

He was the grandson of the physicist,
Henry Lawrence, his name's John Ashbery,
And in his lifetime he did much as an

Editor, teacher and writer.
The other one, that treads the sand behind me,
Is Joe Brainard, who left the world

His memories to read. I'm James Schuyler,
You'll find me in *New American Poetry*,
I'm the one who taught these two to dance.'

If it hadn't been for the burning sand
I'd have run down the bank to greet them;
As things were, I stood awestruck on the track.

Berrigan, my guide, then spoke:
'That's some dance you've got there, James,
Where did you pick that one up,

Is it Italian? This dude is another
Poet, I'm taking him on a tour of Hell,
He's got AHRC funding –

That's like having a Fulbright Scholarship.'
'Is that so?' said Schuyler, 'Now, tell us about
New York, Ted, we were just talking about it.

David Plante, who recently joined our party,
Says it's gone to the dogs. What's the news?'
And Berrigan replied: 'My companion's

Been there more recently than I have,
He should be able to give you the low-down.'
At once I turned red with embarrassment.

If ever I regretted telling a lie
This was the moment.
Berrigan had asked me if

I'd ever been to the US, and ashamed
To admit I hadn't, I'd said,
                                    er,

I recently went to New York.
Now my fib was coming back to haunt me
And I was going to have to bullshit my way out.

'Well,' I began, all of them hanging on
My every word, 'I don't know the city very well,
To tell the truth,

I've only been there for
                        a long weekend,
But from what I hear people are a little

Bit jumpy since 9/11. And
The village isn't what it used to be,
I'm told, it's been taken over by

People in marketing and the media,
The new bourgeoisie,
And the artists have been priced out.'

I blurted out the words without thinking,
My mouth moving without my brain engaged,
As one does when asked a question at a conference.

'Oh my God,' said Brainard, 'it's just like David says.
If you always answer questions this easily,
Poet, then you're a happy man!

Now listen, if you manage to get out of this
Place alive, and return to gaze on the
Beauteous stars, see that you speak of us to men.'

Then they broke up their wheel and fled across
The sand, and as they fled
Their nimble legs seemed like wings in flight.

When they were out of sight, Berrigan turned to
Depart, and I followed, close behind.
We had not gone very far along the track

Before our senses were overwhelmed with
The clanking of loud machinery,
As one hears outside the town of Carrara,

Or on the industrial estate at Harlow,
Yet as we advanced, now along a tarmac
Track, we soon found ourselves

Treading the rim of a vast and bottomless
Pit gouged into the earth
Without pity.

Here no trees grew, nor any scrub, and what remained
Of the earth was scorched and burned up;
Everywhere dust blew about

Whipped by a spiralling wind which
Rose from the depths of the pit.
Along the rim, a few houses still clung on,

Their gardens already devoured by the chasm.
When we had taken in our new surroundings,
Berrigan led me along a narrow spit of land

Flanked by the void on either side,
Which took us to a small island perched above
The hollow, where a few gravestones stood,

And the burning remains of a church.
I wore a bum-flap, clipped to my jeans,
Which I kept about me as a lucky charm,

And here Berrigan turned towards me
And asked me to unclip it; I did as
He suggested, then he hurled it out far into

The abyss, and winking: 'It's as I thought –
A punk and his bum-flap are soon parted,'
He said. 'Now watch!'

It's always better to hold one's tongue
In circumstances where if you speak nobody's
Going to believe you anyway, and I guess

That's why Berrigan kept his silence now.
But that's no reason for my poem to
Shut up too. Reader, I swear to you,

I saw this giant spectre, it was like
A colossal jellyfish, or an airship, *swimming*
Through the smoke-filled air from the depths

Of the pit – it held its arms out like tentacles.

CANTO XVII

'Steady,' said Berrigan, 'don't lose your nerve.
This creature which you behold swimming up
From the quarry pit, with its arms outstretched

In supplication, is no enemy, nor is
It an evil spirit – it's the soul of
The trees which were desecrated to make

This eyesore, in the face of local opposition.
Even Swampy couldn't have put a stop
To this development, so rapacious

Are the quarry company and their backers.
Here profit is the only good, and here
You see the results of that philosophy,

Which no scorched earth policy could match.'
These were the words I heard Berrigan speak
As he beckoned the creature to come ashore

Near the end of the rocky promontory.
The gentle creature, its eyes full of pain
And sorrow, came onward, landing its head

And trunk, but drew not its roots upon the bank.
Its face was like that of a mother who
Has lost all her children in some catastrophe

Yet it shone from inside with a glow of
Benediction; within its translucent head no
Brain matter, but the ghostly silhouettes of trees.

As at times fishing boats lie on the shore,
Moored part on water and part on land,
Or as the endangered beaver, once common

On the polluted banks of the Rhine
In the land of the rowdy *bierkellers*,
Squats to hide from its persecutors,

Just so this great creature lay upon the
Brim of that dusty and bottomless pit.
Berrigan said: 'Let's take a shortcut to

Where the king of limbs has landed.'
Then we made our way down on the right and
Took ten paces towards the edge

Careful to avoid the flames which were falling here.
When we came to the creature, I saw nearby,
Crouched in the burning ruin of the church,

People huddled close to the altar.
Here Berrigan said to me: 'So you can
Get a complete picture of this Zone,

Go over and have a word with them,
But don't hang around; meanwhile I'll have a
Talk with our friend here, and see if we can

Borrow his strong shoulders.' Leaving Berrigan
Behind, I sidled up to these woeful folk,
Sheltering under the narthex.

Their eyes appeared to be bursting with grief;
On this side and on that their hands were flapping
To ward off the flames and the burning flakes

Of sand which rained down on them without let-up.
They were like dogs in summer, plagued by
Fleas that bite them, attacking

Their itch now with snout, now with paw.
When I had examined the faces of
A few of these wretches on whom the flames fell

I couldn't recognise anyone, so burned up
Were their features, but I noticed that each
Wore a singed baseball cap or a T-shirt,

On which I recognised some of the logos,
And these they seemed to wish to protect from
The flames at the expense of all else.

I saw the crest of a blue eagle, a
Black horse, four red triangles arranged to form
A hexagon, a blue and white globe and

A black key; then one who wore a sweatshirt
Stamped with a blue cross surrounded by four
Circles, said: 'What are you doing in this pit?

Didn't you see the KEEP OUT signs?
If you're a protestor, you're too late,
Get out of here! And seeing you're still alive,

You can tell my friend Sir Fred Goodwin
That I have a pew reserved for him right here,
And another one for Peter Cummings,

A lot hotter than his villa on the
Costa del Sol!' Then he made a face, thrusting
His tongue out like a bull that licks its nose.

Not wanting to try Ted's patience, and he'd
Told me to be quick, I hurried back to his side,
Where I found him already saddled up

On the trunk of that great spectre, and he
Said to me: 'I forgot to ask, how's your
Horsemanship? You've read Castiglione,

Now's the time to put your book-learning to the test!'
I climbed up beside him as one who
Reluctantly boards a scary ride at

The funfair, then, putting his arms about
Me, he said: 'Tree spirit, now we're ready,
Take it slowly, be mindful of the living weight

You carry.' As a ferry goes from its mooring
Backwards, so this living airship moved,
And when it felt itself free from the ridge

There where its trunk had been it turned its roots
Which undulated like the tentacles of
An octopus, propelling us over the abyss.

I doubt if Phaethon feared more when he took
The reins of the chariot of the sun,
Scorching the earth as can still be seen today,

Or if Harry Potter was more afraid
The first time he mounted a broomstick
In a game of quidditch, than I was then

When I saw only air on all sides
And saw extinguished every sight
Save the broad back of the king of limbs.

He goes on, swimming slowly, rising up
Like a jumbo jet played back in slow motion,
Then wheels round, changing track,

But I only know this from the wind in my face.
From below, I hear the roar of machinery,
As it scythes into the earth, and at this

I stretch out my neck to look down,
But doing so only made me more apprehensive,
For beneath me I could see nothing but

A city of flames, full of fearful cries
And lamentings, and I drew back tightening
My grip. And then I saw what I had not

Been able to till then: the spiral path
Of our descent, like that of a jet coming in
To Stansted, that has to kill time before

The runway is clear, and as we went down
I saw torment heaped upon torment
Closing in on us from every side.

The tree spirit brought us down gently,
Before a building that resembled a
Multi-storey car park, and here we alighted.

Unburdened, the ghost shot off, like an arrow from a bowstring.

CANTO XVIII

Hell has a stricture called Al's Bulge,
A block of
        ferruginous-hued concrete;

At the gateway of this tottering
Pile is a huge chasm,
           for unread books.

Abandoned by the tree spirit,
        Berrigan walked
Straight in, me behind.

Packed into the dusty foyer,
New misery I see,
        new hands on the whip:

Naked scholars
Stuck in   two-way traffic,
Against us this side, with us that,

Like the ranks when Diana died,
As on one side they queued to sign,
On the other to escape the tide.

Here some queued to take out books,
Others to find them, crammed into
Paternosters, some going up, some down.

On both sides
Librarians in horn-rims
Flayed students fiercely,

Hell, how they made them bleed
In Freshers'
        Week!

Struggling to move, my eyes lit on
One man; immediately I think
'I recognise this one,'

And as I stop to make him out better,
Berrigan, my guide,
                    stops too.

The one with the weals tries to hide,
Lowering his swarthy face; but it's no use,
'Friend,' I say,

'Aren't you he
        who translated our Percy
Into the Conquistadors' noble tongue?'

And he says, 'I grudge telling you;
But your meaning forces me,
It brings me back to old tomes.

I was he who couldn't get enough
Of the wives of friends;
Drawing the beef curtains,

As the smutty story says.
To cover my tracks
                        I kept

A hoover
        in the trunk of my Rover;
Caught in flagrante

I'd dash out   for
My equipment, make out I was
A rep.'

As he speaks
                    the Head Librarian,
A softly-spoken Scot,

    hits him with a lash
    saying, 'Get going, you ogre!
Women aren't meat here.'

In a few steps we reach
        where the paternoster yawns
Below,

Letting the lashed
Go under, into the shit,
That seemed on tap from some sewer.

Rolling a joint, Berrigan points
Towards the
                    stairs,

'See that haughty one,' he says,
'Like a goatherd down from the mountain,
Seeming to scorn any tears at pain?

He's a dude whose skill with myth
Got him inside
                    many knickers.

He hitch-hiked to Lemnos once,
After the first-generation feminists
Had slaughtered their menfolk.

Here his gilded tongue
Tricked Hypsipyle, a young poetess,
And he left her all alone, pregnant.

And over there a little,
                    clawing off the shit,
The one in heels

With the pink leather suit
                    and all the lipstick,
Look closely at that woman's face,

Under the stinking make-up,
                    that's our Professor Emerita,
A hard-nosed Lacanian,

                    whether she's
                              written more books
Or screwed more dons

Is a tough call.'

CANTO XIX

David Willetts, you wanker, and your shit-brained
Followers, pick-pockets in silk suits,
Who play the pimp with HE,

Which should be a right,
                          and free;
Can you imagine being told, age 25,

That you'd got cerebral palsy and the
Treatment would cost you an arm and a leg –
But it's OK, you can defer payment,

Spread it over 20 years, no cause for alarm…
Don't you ever stop
                          to think?

Now, in your honour, let the fire-alarm sound,
For it's here, in Al's Bulge,
'The Pits', as the students call it,

That you and your kind hang out.
Already, we had stopped, to spit on his statue,
When we began to make our way

Up a wide granite stairway.
On the side wall, as we climbed,
I noticed what at first I took for

Some weird art installation,
Something from the Latin American Collection:
Here a series of round holes were

Punched into livid rock. They looked
About as wide and as deep as a manhole,
And from the mouth of each a pair of feet

Stuck out, and legs up to the knee,
And these were twitching frenziedly, as if
Dancing to electropop, like a robot

From *1984*, while on the soles of
The feet a flame too danced, as
Lit brandy on a Christmas pudding.

'I know what you're thinking,' said Berrigan,
'But this is no surrealist montage,
The feet you see sticking out of the wall

Belong to the vice-chancellors
Of the university, the rest of their bodies
Are stuffed inside.'

'Who's that one,' I asked, 'the one
Who's really going for it
                              up ahead?'

'If you really want to know, why don't
You ask him yourself?' said Berrigan.
'*He* can talk.' When we reached the eighth

Or the ninth step, where the stairs begin to turn
To the left, we came up close to the cleft.
'Hello,' I stuttered, 'I can only see your feet,

But if you can hear me, and still have a voice, speak.'
I stood like a holy man confessing some
Hardened assassin on Death Row,

Who, strapped in his chair, calls him back
To delay the moment of death:
The feet stilled, then a voice came out,

Muffled, but audible: 'Is that you on the stair,
Riordan? Here already? The statutes
Were out by several years on your account.

Are you so soon sated with that wealth for which
You made no bones about seizing the university
By deceit, only then to make havoc with her?'

I stood as one in negative equity,
Unsure how to understand what I heard
And uncertain how to reply.

Then Berrigan nudged me, saying:
'Tell him you're not the one he takes you for.'
At which I stepped right up to the hole

And did as he instructed. At this
The shade knotted his feet together,
Sighing in a laboured fashion,

Then in a voice which was half whining,
He said: 'Then what do you want of me?
If you've trudged up these stairs, rather than

Take the paternoster, to know who I am,
Learn that I was once clothed in the great mantle,
But beneath the finery

I was greed incarnate, so eager
To advance my own ends, that up above
I stuffed my pockets, and here am stuffed in one.

I was the one who lobbied for top-up fees,
I shut down any subject area that wasn't
Making a killing, and encouraged those that would

Bring in cash – the EBS was my brainchild, to the arts
I was no friend. Under my head are stuffed all the
Others who came before me, moneygrubbers to a man,

Cowering within the fissures of the rock.
I too will go down there when the one I
Mistook you for retires.

But already I've stood toasting in this
Undignified posture longer than he will,
For after him, from the north, will come

A ruthless shepherd who will liquidate
All of the humanities, a man who will
Put our deeds in the shade.

He'll be another John Brooks:
If he doesn't shut you down, he'll either
Pension you off or make you work longer hours.'

He rambled on and on, like one who enjoyed
The sound of his own voice and was used
To his audience hanging on every word.

Perhaps I spoke out of turn, but I answered
Him with what was upmost in my mind:
'While your salaries can be counted in

Hundreds of thousands,
                              have you any
                     idea how much we pay our TAs?

And do you know how much the cleaners earn,
Who even have to pay to park at work?
Do you know what we pay poets?

Stay stuck where you are, for you've got exactly
What you deserve; your avarice grieves the world,
And your vision of a chrestomathic university

Chained to markets and so-called creative industries
Leaves no room for thought, and cares nothing for
The rubbished margins of your success story.

It's you and your like who have put the "vice"
In "vice-chancellor", you should be ashamed.'
And as I ranted on at him like this,

Like I do when I'm completely pissed,
Whether it was through rage,
Or because he had a bad conscience,

His feet kicked out violently at the air.
I think Berrigan dug what I said,
For all the while he couldn't stop grinning.

Then he gave me a big bear-hug,
Crushing me against his broad chest,
And holding me like this, he lifted me up,

And didn't let go until we'd reached
The top of the stairwell, where he put me
Down by a glass cabinet containing

Some pamphlets by Tom Raworth, *Lion Lion*,
Haiku, *From the Hungarian*, then after
We'd looked at these for some minutes Berrigan

Turned to me and said: 'Let's split.'

CANTO XX

Now I must make punishment into poetry
To make the matter of the twentieth canto
Of the first chant, the one about the fallen.

Already, we had reached that spot from where
You can peer down into the pit of Al's Bulge;
The floor, here, was sticky with tears,

And walking between the rows of books
Near Sociology and Demographics
I saw people go silent and weeping,

Like a funeral procession in our world.
When my sight descended lower on them
I saw that each was strangely distorted:

Their faces were twisted so that their chins
Rested on their backbones, and they shuffled backwards
To go forwards, gazing down at their own buttocks.

Perhaps there was a case of Freud's – some forgotten
Hysteric whose hang-ups expressed themselves so,
But none that I've heard of.

Reader, if the theorists are correct, you
Need to be active in the construction of the text,
So imagine for yourself whether or not

I could keep my eyes dry, when I saw the
Human form so twisted, that weeping eyes
Streamed down to wash their own arses.

I wept, I couldn't help myself, since having
A child I've gone soft like that.
I had to sit down next to one of the

Computer terminals, then Berrigan said:
'Quit blubbing, the shades in this hole
Aren't worth your tears, they're mostly

Folk who were so tied up with growth charts
Or tea leaves they couldn't see
What was happening in their own back yards.

Lift your head up, right up, see the
Seismologist for whom the earth
Split wide open while on a research trip

In Haiti. "Where you rushing off to
Doctor?" they cried, as he ran for home;
He kept running till he fell into a crevice

And into the hands of Landman, who gets them all.
See how he makes a chest of his back: because
He wished to see too far ahead he goes backwards.

And look, there's Tiresias, the old devil,
You'll have heard of him, he changed himself
From man to woman, altering his bits,

And later, he had to strike two serpents
Coiled together in the grass with his rod,
So that he could resume his man form.

The next one, with her back facing
Tiresias' belly, is Mystic Meg,
She was a graduate in English at

The University of Leeds who claimed
To possess psychic powers – but she
Didn't predict the Yorkshire Ripper.

And that one with her long red hair
Covering her breasts, and with her hairy
Parts protruding behind her, was Providence,

Who searched through many lands before
She ended up where I was born; let
Me tell you a little about her history.

After the death of her father, it's said, she found
Herself alone and with a child in New England;
At that time single mothers were hunted down

Like witches, so she fled into the wilderness
Living for some years in the heart of a swamp
Where she dwelt amongst the Narragansett Indians,

Learning how to treat sickness with natural
Medicines, and how to tell when cold was coming.
Here her daughter secretly married a chieftain,

But they were discovered, then banished, and with the
Mother and some servants they set up a new
Settlement beyond the boundaries of the marsh,

Where the land was uncultivated and
Naked of inhabitants, declaring it a
Place of religious freedom and offering

Equal treatment to Indians and white folk.
There she stopped to practise her arts,
And there she lived

                        till her 130th year,
When her soul took leave of the earth
And left her body vacant.

Afterwards, they built a city over her
Dead bones, and in memory of her who
First chose the place, they named it Providence.

And now, swear to me, if you ever hear
The origin of my city described otherwise,
Don't let tall tales rob you of the truth.'

And I replied: 'Berrigan, I don't
Believe a word of it, you're pulling my
Leg, aren't you?' And he did not reply,

But let out a loud belly laugh instead.
'Now tell me,' I said, 'no joking, who
Are these shades passing us now,

Are any of them people I should know?'
'That one,' he said to me, 'with the white beard
Falling down his backbone, was a climate

Scientist at UEA, who by fiddling
His data brought just science into disrepute,
You might have seen his story in the papers.

That other one, with the skinny legs,
Was an academic at Carnegie who
Predicted robots would be in every

Household by the mid-1980s.
Behind him is the man who said of rock'n'roll
In 1955: "It will be gone by June."

And look, this wretched crowd taking up the rear,
They were all women from Essex,
Most of them guilty of nothing but owning a pet,

Tried by Matthew Hopkins for witchcraft,
Then hanged – the methods that dude used would
Raise eyebrows at Guantanamo.

The procession is endless, but come,
We need to get moving, believe me, there
Are plenty more shades for you to meet yet.

Quick, let's jump into the paternoster
Which will take us to our next port of call.'
And then Berrigan stepped towards the lift shaft,

And when the right moment came, grabbing me, leapt.

CANTO XXI

As we reached the top of the paternoster
I saw the red sign warning us to alight –
'Don't worry about that,' said Berrigan,

As we lurched on, into the darkness.
When the lift reached the highest point of
Its trajectory, it began to go down once more,

And just as it did so a door appeared
Which I hadn't noticed before. I'd scarcely
Had time to read the words NO ENTRY,

When Berrigan shoved me through it
Then jumped in behind,
As the paternoster continued its course:

The place we came to was strangely dark.
On the waterfront at Wivenhoe,
Just down from the Rose and Crown,

Lies a busy boatyard, where in winter
They boil the dark brown pitch to caulk their boats;
As they cannot sail, here, between pints, they toil:

Some build new boats, bending the planks into
Shape with steam, others repair old ones,
Plugging the broken boards

                  with fibreglass,
Some hammer at the prow, some at the stern,
Some make oars, some mend the sails.

Here, too, but heated by a thermoelectric
Ring, not a camping gas, a sticky brown soup
Boiled away in an industrial-sized vat,

All smeared round the rim with sticky residue.
I peered into it, but saw nothing there,
Only the huge bubbles, which rose and fell.

I was standing there, gazing fixedly into
The soup, when Berrigan shouted: 'Watch out!'
Then pulled me to him from where I stood.

As I turned round, I saw behind us,
Cruising along the rim, a caterer,
Winged, dressed in black. He looked scary,

Like someone you wouldn't want to mess with,
His wings outstretched as he skimmed over the broth.
'Now you can see,' said Berrigan, 'the raw

Recruits for the new Catering College.'
On one of his hunched shoulders, this one carried
A young student from the summer school.

He shouted out from above the soup: 'Hey!
Kitchen Devils! Here's one of Saint Zita's
Children, you know, the exchange students from Lucca,

You shove him under while I go back for more.
They really are a bunch of Mafiosi, this lot,
They'll do anything for a backhander,

Except their tutor, Paolo, of course – he wouldn't
Let me touch them until I offered him
Some free luncheon vouchers.'

He flung him in, then wheeled off over the soup;
I've never seen a police dog move so fast,
Not even to catch a G7 protester.

The student plunged in, head first,
Then rose to the surface, waving his arms about
As he tried to come up for air.

'No backstroke allowed in this pool!' cried one
Of the Kitchen Devils, 'You're not in the
Serchio now! Unless you want to feel

Our forks, I'd stay under the surface, mate!'
Then they all jabbed him with their prongs,
Like scullery boys poking the meat into

The pot to keep it near the flame.
Berrigan said: 'You'd better keep a low profile
And let me do the talking, otherwise

They might want to throw you into the pot –
It's a long time since they had fresh meat.'
He left me crouching behind a pile of old

Cookbooks, as he stepped forward to talk to them.
With all the noise and ferocity of guard dogs
Rushing out on an unsuspecting rambler,

The Kitchen Devils surrounded Berrigan,
Turning against him all their crooks.
But Berrigan stood his ground, and said:

'Hold it right there, you're wasting your time
If you think you're going to hook me –
Who's in charge here? Let me have a word with them.'

They all cried: 'Jamie, he wants you!'
At which one stepped forward from their midst.
This one had no wings and wore a checked shirt,

Saying: 'Sorry, guv'nor, but you've entered
A restricted area – only
Catering students are allowed down here.'

'Look,' said Berrigan, losing his patience,
'Do you really think I'd have gotten this far
Without recommendation from the top? Our trip

Has approval from the Dean, from the VC,
And we have funding from the AHRC,
What more do you want?'

At this, all his bravado collapsed,
The ladle he carried, too, fell to his feet,
And he said to the others: 'Hands off this one!'

Now, Berrigan called me from my
Hiding place, yet as I stepped towards him,
From the movements they made, and from the

Looks on their faces, I was worried they
Would break their pact. I was reminded of
A photograph I had seen of de Valera's

Men on the day they surrendered,
And the worried looks on their faces
As they marched past the Brits.

I drew up near to Berrigan, my guide,
Keeping a close watch on the under-chefs.
They fingered their prongs, saying:

'Shall I give him one up the arse?'
And 'Why don't we show him the carvery?'
But Jamie, who spoke with my guide, turned round

And said: 'You lot, behave! Or you're out of here!'
Then he turned to us, saying: 'If you're
Trying to find your way out of the kitchens

You're heading the wrong way – the fire exit's blocked.
If you want to get out you'll need to walk round
This vat of soup and go through the café.

I'm sending a few of my apprentices that way
To deliver the new menus – they can show you
The way, they won't mess you about again,

Not after what I've said to them.'
At that point Jamie began to call out
Orders: 'Right – Wings, Hogswash, over here,

Itchy, Dogbreath, put those pans down, you're
Going with them. Mothballs, you're in charge,
Take them to the café, along with the menus,

And don't get lost. Curly, Frosty, Windbutt,
Pisspants, Sniveller – take a box of menus each
And careful you don't drop them in the soup!'

Worried, I turned to Berrigan, asking:
'Can't we go on our own? Surely you know
The way? Don't you see how they're grinding

Their teeth – I'm sure they're up to something.'
But Berrigan brushed my worries aside,
Saying: 'Let them grind away.

They're just doing it to frighten the students
Cooking in the soup – it's not our worry.'
As they started off round the broth, each one

Blew a raspberry, and Jamie signalled back in kind.

CANTO XXII

I have heard the bagpipes played at the Edinburgh
Tattoo, I have heard the Orangemen blow their flutes
On the twelfth of July, I have watched

Military funerals roll by to the beat of
A drum, I have heard the hunter's horn sounded
In Mahler's First Symphony, a gong beat at

Dinnertime, a buzzer ring when my pizza's ready,
But I never heard a fanfare quite as strange
As the bugling of these Kitchen Devils.

We moseyed along with the ten chefs by
Our side, we were in bad company, but
As the old saying has it: 'With saints in

The church, with boozers in the tavern.'
As we went I kept my eyes glued to the
Soup vat, to see what the deal was in this pit.

As dolphins arch their backs leaping through the
Waves in the Bay of Biscay, as they come out
To greet the latest ferry from Portsmouth,

So now and then, to ease the pain, some student
Stuck in the broth poked his back above the surface,
Then dived under again as quick as lightning.

And as frogs sit with their muzzles poking out
Round the edge of a pond or a ditch,
So the students here gathered at the vat's rim,

But as Mothballs drew near they dunked their heads
In the soup. One of them was a bit slower
Than the rest, just as often one frog lingers

A little longer at the pond's edge, and I
Saw – it still makes me sick thinking about it –
Itchy, who was standing level with him,

Stick his hook into his shoulder and yank
Him out, turning him about in the air:
He looked just like the Orford Merman.

By this point I'd got their names by heart,
For I'd listened carefully when they were picked,
And listened carefully now as they called out.

'Hey, Sniveller, dig your claws into his back
And peel the skin off him!' some of them shouted.
And I: 'Berrigan, if you can,

Find out who that sucker is
        who has fallen into the hands
                of his adversaries.'

Berrigan strode over to the side of the vat,
Beneath where he dangled in the air,
And asked him where he was from.

'I was born,' he replied proudly, 'in Gosport, Hampshire,
My father sent me to Alverstoke, I
Graduated at Trinity Hall;

Later, I became an MP, that's where
I learned my graft: perhaps you've heard about
The pond feature I claimed for,

That was my finest hour, a floating duck island,
Worth nearly two grand.
Now I pay my bills by boiling in this soup.'

Then Dogbreath, who had two canines jutting
Out from his mouth, like a fox,
Let him feel how just one of them could rip the flesh:

The duck had fallen into the hands of the foxes.
Yet Mothballs grabbed him now in an armlock,
Saying: 'Hold off now, while I have him pinned.'

Then turning to us, he added: 'If you've
Any more questions, you'd better ask them quick,
Before the rest of the lads get stuck in.'

And so Berrigan, my guide, asked: 'Do you
Know if there are any from Essex
Simmering in there beside you?'

'From Essex?' he replied, 'You've got more than
Your fair share in here, I can tell you, you're
Top of the league tables for grafting.

Just a moment ago, I was talking to
One of them, I wish I was still with him now,
Then I wouldn't have these prongs to worry about.'

Then Windbutt cried out: 'OK, we've waited
Long enough!" And with a meat hook he ripped
Into the muscles round his upper arm,

Tearing off a lump of flesh. Sniveller, too,
Was keen to join in the fun, taking a swing
At the MP's legs, but now Mothballs

Wheeled round, giving them the evils.
When they'd laid off, Berrigan, my guide,
Began to question the wretch, who still gazed

At his fresh wound. 'Who's the one from Essex,'
He asked, 'that you left behind in the soup?'
'Tucker,' he said, 'a vicar from Basildon,

Bent as a ten-bob note – he took bribes from
Inmates at Wormwood Scrubs to put in
A good word for them. He hangs out with

The Professor, a retired maths don at
The university, notorious
For fiddling his research expenses.

Go away! Look how he's licking his lips!
I could tell you more, but I'm scared that one's
About to take a slice out of me.'

But then Mothballs rounded on Curly, whose
Wild eyes showed he was about to strike,
And shouted: 'Hands off, you old soup stirrer!'

'If you want to see some Essex boys,'
The frightened shade resumed,
'I can call some over,

But the Kitchen Devils will have to back off
Or they'll be afraid to surface –
All I need do is whistle,

That's our signal when the coast is clear.'
Pisspants let out a loud laugh and shook his head:
'We're not going to fall for that old chestnut, mate,'

He said, 'we weren't born yesterday.'
'So you don't fancy some Essex rump, then?'
Said the MP. 'Enough,' chipped in Wings,

Who couldn't resist the challenge.
'Call them up! But if you make a run for it,
Be warned, I'll not come after you on legs,

But flying through the air with this meat hook!'
The Kitchen Devils all stood back from the
Vat, jumping down from the rim,

And the first to do so was Pisspants,
Who had been so against it
                                            from the start.

The MP's sense of timing didn't let him down –
He leapt
                                            and was gone.

The Kitchen Devils were all pissed off,
None more so than Wings
Who'd given the MP the nod,

'Just you wait, you wanker,' he cried,
'I'm coming for you!' And at that he flew
Off and dive-bombed the soup

Swinging his hook into its depths,
But there was nothing doing –
The minister had vanished in the brew.

Wings was now stuck in the vat himself
Yelling out for help. Frosty, who was nearest,
Just laughed, and rather than offer him a hand,

Poked him under with his prong, calling:
'Come and get it! Deep-fried Devil!'
But Wings was in no mood for joking,

And with a yank on the fork had his
Companion in the soup beside him.
They began to wrestle with each other

Digging their claws into the flesh,
But quickly the heat made them separate,
'Help!' they cried, 'We're burning!'

To put an end to the sorry mess
Mothballs sent a party to the rescue:
They flew over the soup

Stretching their forks and their ladles out to
The simmering chefs, who were already
Scalded within the crust.

We slipped off while they were still at it.

CANTO XXIII

Silent, apart, and without escort
We went on, the one before, the other
After, as haiku writers on a long journey.

I was trying to explain to Ted how the whole thing
Reminded me of a fable of Aesop's,
The one where a frog offers to take a mouse

Over a river, but ends up drowning it,
Finally getting eaten itself, by a
Passing kite – the more I talked the less

Convinced he looked – when, one thought leading to
Another, as sometimes happens,
The whole thing suddenly came clear to me:

'It's not like what we just saw, it's like *us*:
You're the frog, I'm the mouse, the Kitchen Devils
Are the hawk: to put it bluntly,

We're in danger, because after what we
Made them do, and everything that happened,
They're going to be pretty pissed off with us!'

I was so frightened I kept glancing back
Over my shoulder; but now Berrigan
Looked more convinced: 'I get your drift,' he said,

'We'd better split.' Berrigan had scarcely finished
Outlining his plan when I heard them coming,
Wings spread, intent on catching us.

He grabbed me by the arm instinctively,
Like a mother waking to the sound of a smoke alarm
Who pulls her son close to her and runs

Without even a thought of getting dressed,
And we dashed out through the café, leaving behind us
A trail of upturned tables and spilt cappuccinos.

No sooner were we outside than Berrigan
Turned to me, saying: 'Hold on!'
Then we both leapt down the scree

We had descended once before,
This time sliding down on our backsides
Like kids on a hill walk when the snow comes down.

We landed with a bump in the underground
Car park, next to a door marked CAST ONLY.
As we looked back up the slope we could see

The Kitchen Devils waving their prongs,
But they didn't dare follow us,
We were out of their jurisdiction.

Within we found a painted crowd, who walked
Round at a snail's pace on a raised stage,
Weeping, their look worn-out.

They wore huge cloaks which, on the outside, shone like
Gold, like something you might see on a catwalk,
But inside they were of lead, so heavy

That by comparison a suit of armour
Would have seemed as flimsy as a shellsuit.
At first I thought we had interrupted

The rehearsals for some Beckett play,
And I turned to Berrigan and said:
'Is it some new interpretation of *Quad*?'

But Berrigan, my guide, motioned with his head,
As though to say 'If only...', then added:
'See if there's anyone you recognise.'

I looked up at them from where I stood in
The pit as they trudged slowly by,
Then one of their number, who saw me gazing,

Called out: 'You, who seem to move so freely
In the dark air, perhaps you have come
To be fitted with a cloak?'

Berrigan told me to stay still, and as I
Continued to gaze on the gilded shades
I saw two who showed by their look

Great eagerness to be with me,
But their heavy load held them back.
When at last they drew up alongside us

They looked at me for a long time
Without uttering a word, then they turned to
One another and said between them:

'By the way he moves his throat, I'd say
This one was alive; and if they are dead
By what right do they go without the heavy stole?'

Then they said to me: 'Breather, for that is
What you seem to be, welcome to the Hedge School
Of the hypocrites. Tell us who you are?'

And I to them: 'On the slimy banks of
The Lagan I was born and grew up in that
Strife-torn city, and I am in the body

That I always had. But tell me, who are you
Who distil such sorrow as I see running
Down your cheeks? And what punishment is it

That shines so brightly on your backs?'
And one of them replied to me: 'Our gilded cloaks
Are lined with lead so thick that it makes us

Creak as we walk. We are from the ranks of
Hypocritical academics, who did not practise
What we preached: my name was Jeremy,

I was a well-known Marxist historian
Who sent my son to a fee-paying school
To give him a head start; my friend here was

Once a famous theorist, a translator
Of Derrida, espousing radical politics,
Who treated all she met with scorn.'

'I know your type…' I began, but said no more,
For now my eyes fell on one crucified
On the stage with three stakes driven into the ground,

And when he caught sight of me he writhed all over,
Blowing into his beard with sighs,
And Jeremy, who witnessed this, said:

'That impaled figure you see stretched out
In pain is the man who advised the VC
To raise the fees to £9,000 a year.

Naked, he lies stretched out across our path,
As you can see, and as we pass over him,
He must feel the weight of our heavy cloaks.'

I saw Berrigan staring contemptuously
At this forlorn figure, stretched out on the stage,
The one who had raised fees now unable to raise a hand.

Afterwards, Berrigan addressed the
Historian: 'Tell me, buddy,' he said,
'Is there any way out of this place

That doesn't go through the café?
We had a bit of a disagreement
With some of the catering students.'

'I can show you out through the green room,
If you like,' the Marxist replied,
'From there you should be able to scramble

Up to Square 5, from where it's a short walk
To the next pit. It would be impossible
Wearing these heavy cloaks, but you two,

Who are light on your feet, should make it.'
At the thought of the climb Berrigan looked
Peeved, and let out an exaggerated sigh.

We left the Hedge School behind with heavy footsteps.

CANTO XXIV

In that part of the youthful year, when the
Hoarfrost copies his white sister's imprint
On soil, image that soon fades,

The farmer, down on hay, looks out over his
Fields, and curses; but after a power shower,
When he looks out again, he sees the grass is green

And with a spring in his step he heads to the 4x4;
Just so, Berrigan made me lose heart
When I heard him sighing, but just as quick

He whipped out the plaster to heal my wound;
For when we reached the foot of the mountain
Of rubble he smiled and threw me a rope.

With this I clipped myself to him, then we
Began the ascent, moving carefully from
One slab to the next, Berrigan in front,

Me behind; pulling me towards the top
Of a great splinter of concrete, he said:
'Now grab hold of this ridge, but test it first

To see if it will take your weight.'
This was no road for gilded cloaks,
For though I had Berrigan to guide me,

And he had the weight of a shade,
We struggled to mount from crag to crag
Without crampons or hexes.

When we came to the point where the last stone
Breaks off, I was so sweaty and puffed out
That I couldn't take a step more.

Yet no sooner had I sat down
Than Berrigan began to take the piss:
'Get up off your backside, academic,' he said.

'I'm a fifty-year-old man,' I replied,
'What you going to do about it?'
'Nobody,' he said, 'ever won fame that way.'

And at that he gave me his hand and yanked
Me to my feet; I stretched and puffed my chest out,
Trying to look as if I was up for it,

Then we took off with heavy steps towards
A large building that shone brightly in the
Darkness, traversing a narrow bridge.

As we went I made an effort to speak
So as not to seem faint, whereat a voice
Rose up from the pit beneath the bridge,

Though what it said I couldn't make out,
It was like the voice of a man running at speed.
I peered over the side of the bridge

But saw nothing in the gloom, so I said:
'Master, why don't we slip round the end there,
where the grass is worn away, and look into the pit?'

'Nice idea,' he said, 'lead on.'
From the centre of the bridge, we came to
The point where it ends and joins a steep bank,

And from this vantage point the pit opened up
To me: down there I saw a terrifying confusion
Of literary agents, all wearing name tags,

Double-barrelled, triple-barrelled, quadruple-
Barrelled, all of such a monstrous girth
Even now the thought of them makes my blood run cold.

Let the Libyan desert boast no more, for
Though it engenders chelydri and jaculi,
Phareans, cenchres and double-headed amphisbenes,

It never spawned so great a plague of venom,
Not even if you added the whole of Egypt
And all the lands of the Arab spring.

Amidst this cruel power-dressing swarm
Were authors running, naked and shit-scared,
Without hope of *pied-à-terre* or invisibility cloak.

They had their hands tied behind their backs with contracts,
And their loins were all disfigured and bloated
With the size of their advances.

Just then, an author ran straight past us –
An agent shot out and clamped her teeth there
Where the neck is bound upon the shoulders.

No Mills and Boon was ever written so
Quickly as he took fire, burned up,
And collapsed into a heap of ashes,

Which fell like leaves onto a carpet of
Unsolicited manuscripts, where some of the
Best work of its time lay rotting and neglected.

After he had been incinerated like this,
The ash particles reunited themselves
And he resumed his former shape

(Just so, as J.K. Rowling informs us,
The phoenix dies and then is born again
When it approaches its five-hundredth year).

As a man suffering a stroke or a heart
Attack will fall, and knows not why
(Perhaps high blood pressure, stress, cigarettes,

Or a failed marriage, drags him down, or some
Impure line of coke chokes his vital spirits),
Then, scrambling to his feet, will look around

All bewildered by the great anguish he
Has undergone, such was this author when he rose.
Berrigan asked who he was and he answered:

'It's not that long ago, though God it seems it,
That I rained down from Hull into this fierce gullet.
I loved the bachelor pad more than human

Intercourse, preferred to stay at home with
A packet of fags and a bottle of whisky
Than spend an evening down the pub

Exchanging polite chat, preferred a
Magazine to a real woman –
Less trouble at the end of the day.'

I said to Berrigan: 'Tell him not to budge,
My mother once worked with him in the
Library at Queen's, ask him what he's doing here.'

But the poet heard very well what I said,
And didn't try to hide it; he turned towards me,
Coughed, and with a look of guilt, said:

'That you have caught me by surprise in this
Wretched pit pains me more than the day
I kicked the bucket, for that's something you can't help.

But I'll answer what you ask: I'm stuck in this
Hell-hole for stealing a library book when I
Was at Oxford – largely so Amis couldn't

Get his hands on it. There – not even Motion
Knows about that. Some might say I'm here
Because I narrowed the scope of poetry,

But that's poppycock. I don't want you to
Rejoice over the fact you bumped into me
In this pit if you ever get out of here

Alive, so prick up your ears and drink in
My prophecy: *The Arts Council will strip*
Poetry publishers of all their miserable

Grants, and the one who publishes your books
Will be the first to go under. After that
There'll be no room in the market for

Anything more elevated than Pam Ayres!'

CANTO XXV

When he had finished delivering his speech,
Larkin stuck his two fingers up at us,
Shouting: 'This be the prophecy!'

And now the agents became my friends, for one
Of them, a blonde, coiled herself round his neck
And started tonguing him, which shut him up for good,

While another, a brunette, coming from the front,
Entwined him in her arms so that
He could barely move a muscle.

Coventry, you crappest of crap towns,
Wasn't it enough to give us Philip Larkin?
Did you really have to follow that star turn

With Paul Connew and Hazel O'Connor,
King, Dennis Spicer and Pete Waterman?
Will you not be content till you have ruined

Every art form? Losing his balance under
The attention of the agents, Larkin collapsed.
'Berrigan,' I said, 'tell me something about

The shades in this pit, what brings them together?'
'This pit,' explained Berrigan, 'contains thieves,
As Larkin said – but the worst crimes you'll see

Punished here are crimes against literature,
That's why the agents are here, as well as
Larkin, and some other Movement poets.

Just as literary agents, in their pursuit
Of an ever-wider readership, and ever
Increasing sales, reduce all writing to a

Commodity, and a formula, so Movement
Writers reduce all poetry to the
Formulaic: journey, minor epiphany, return.

So it's fitting the two groups come together here:
The writers have their identities robbed by agents,
But the agents are made to suffer in their turn,

As these Movement poets are the ones who never move.'
Just then a cleaner darted past, shouting:
'Where's he gone to, that bald librarian?

I found some more mags in his room, hidden
Under the Auden.' Not even the Hôtel de Nesle
Had as many cockroaches as she had on her back,

There was a giant one crouched on her shoulders,
Just behind the neck, with its wings outstretched,
That seemed poised to take a bite out of her.

Berrigan said to me: 'That one's Dolores,
She's down here rather than with her mates
Because of all the stuff she stole from the

Store cupboard, mostly wine and Rancheros.'
As he was talking the cleaner passed out of sight,
Then right under our noses three shades appeared

Which neither of us would have noticed,
If they hadn't cried out: 'Who are *you*?'
I couldn't recognise any of them,

But it happened, as it sometimes does by chance,
That one of them addressed another:
'Where did your friend go, Thwaity?'

And then, to stop Berrigan from opening
His mouth, I put my finger to my lips,
Hoping they might say more.

Reader, if you're reluctant to believe
What I'm about to tell you, that's no surprise:
I hardly credit it myself, and I was there.

I was still looking at them when a black
Triple-barrelled agent, a New Yorker with a
Six-figure contract, darted up in front of

One of them and fastened herself upon him.
With the middle finger of one hand she teased
The author's locks, with the other she grabbed

His neck and kissed him on both cheeks.
She then spread her legs and rubbed herself
Against the author's thighs, stuffing the

Contract between his legs. Ivy was never
Rooted to a tree as round the author's limbs
The agent entwined her own;

Then they stuck together, as if they had been
Heat-bonded, mingling their colours,
So that neither seemed what they had been at first,

Just as a brown tint, ahead of the flame,
Will advance across the white pages
Of a pile of burning manuscripts.

The other two looked on and each cried:
'Oh dear, Andrew! If you could only see how you're
Changing, you don't look yourself!'

The two heads, already large, merged into
One gigantic one, and the features of each
Face combined together till neither was recognisable,

Rather they looked like a face made in a potato.
The four arms grew together to make two,
Then the thighs, bellies, chests and feet

Mixed together to sprout such members as were
Never seen before in hospital or freak show
Or photographs by Diane Arbus.

The former shape was all extinct in them:
Both and neither the perverse image seemed,
And such it limped away with slow step.

Just then, at the speed of a darting lizard,
Another agent, she was short with fiery hair
And a fuck-off belt, came charging towards

The two remaining authors. She shot up
And sank her teeth into one of them,
Right on middle stump, then fell down,

Stretched out before him, only to jump up at once,
Offering him a Balkan Sobranie.
They both began to smoke languidly,

Staring at each other, the author seemingly
Lost for words, blowing smoke into each
Other's faces, their feet motionless.

Let Marie Darrieussecq from now on be silent
With her stories about changing into a pig,
And Ovid too can shut up about Cadmus

And Arethusa – he may have changed one
Into a snake and the other into a fountain,
But does my face look bothered?

He never transformed two creatures standing
Face to face so that each took on the features
Of the other: a change of perfect symmetry.

The agent split her tongue into a fork,
While the author drew his legs together,
As if he were standing to attention to receive

The Presidential Medal of Freedom;
His legs and thighs along with them so stuck
To each other that the join became invisible,

While the cloven tongue swelled out growing feet
Which hardened at their extremities to form toes.
Now the legs drew back into the body softening

And growing furry, as they took on the features
The agent had shed, while her pubis
Thrust out to make the member old men piss through.

The smoke from each was now swirling round the
Other, exchanging shape and complexion,
Hair growing on one who had none before,

The other balding before my very eyes,
The one's pale flat chest filling out with young breasts,
The other's youth collapsing into withered age.

The one rose up, the other sank, but neither
Let up staring right back at the other,
Fixed eye to eye as they swapped faces.

When the smoke had cleared I saw the one transformed
Into the body of the author shuffle off
As if in a pair of slippers, muttering:

'Let Conquest now creep about at
Literary lunches on all fours
                        as I had to do.'

Just so I saw the cargo of the pit of thieves
Change and exchange form, and if my pen lets me down,
May the strangeness of it all excuse me.

But though my eyes could scarcely believe what they saw,
And my mind was sore perplexed,
I could still see clearly enough to notice

The one of the three who stood there alone
And was not changed, and if I am not
Mistaken, now I think on it, it bore a

Striking resemblance to Blake Morrison.

CANTO XXVI

Rejoice, Oxford, since you are so powerful
That over sea and fen you beat your wings,
And your name spreads through Hell itself.

I was shocked to find amongst the thieves,
Where those condemned for crimes against literature
Dwell, three of your alumni, a circumstance

That does you little credit.
Not content with taking over parliament
Now you wish to police literature with your

Agents and keep it safe with your unmagnanimous
Authors and their self-important posturings.
But literature is no coterie,

And if history is anything to go by,
Laureates
                              do not last.

We quit the pit of thieves,
Zone 8 Area G, making our way
Up some scree down which we had come.

To climb back up we had to get down
On our hands and knees, pursuing our
Solitary way, for here foot without hand sped not.

Once at the top, we took a shortcut up some stairs,
And came via a devious route, past some ducks
Hunkered down in a muddy tyre track,

As in a poem by Thomas Hardy,
To the LTB, where many lost souls
Stood about conversing and smoking.

It filled me with grief, and fills me with grief
Again now, when I think back on what I saw,
And as I write I know I must not indulge

My pen, but tell it straight, as it is,
For if some bit of luck, or something better,
Has gifted me this good, I don't want to abuse it.

As headline acts (in the season when rock
Festivals fill the farmers' fields with litter,
And shepherds take their annual leave)

Look out into the gathering darkness
To see the flickering of lighters
Held aloft, with flames just as numerous

The chasm of Zone 8 Area H was lit up.
I was standing by the bridge, on the long
Tiled seating area, leaning over

The opaque glass screen, so far over that
If Berrigan had not held my legs I might
Have toppled below. At first I thought there

Was some chemistry experiment going
On outdoors, perhaps involving explosives,
Until I remembered chemistry had been shut down.

Berrigan, reading my thoughts, was quick to
Put me right: 'Those are no Bunsen burners,'
He said, 'within these moving flames are souls,

And each is burned by its own conscience.'
'If that's the case,' I said, 'then who is in that fire
Which splits in two at its tip,

Like that flame which, if Graves speaks truly,
Sprang up once from the funeral
Pyre of Oedipus' warring sons?'

'Within,' said Berrigan, my guide, 'lie the
Souls of Peter Hulme and David Musselwhite,
Suffering in anger with each other,

Over the direction the department should take.
Poetic justice makes them walk together now.
Inside the flame they lament the compromises

That let The Enlightenment course fall by the wayside,
And led languages to all but disappear.'
'Master,' I said, 'if the souls within these flames

Can speak, please, can we have a word with them now?
I never quarrelled with either of these just men,
And hold them both in high esteem,

The one for his work on Columbus and
Postcolonialism, the other for his
Work on Hardy and the phantasmatic.'

'I can understand why you'd want to speak
With these two,' said Berrigan, 'and I'm not
Going to stand in your way, but hold your tongue,

Let me do the talking, for I can guess
What you want to ask, and perhaps, since they
Were hispanists, they would not pay attention

To your words with the respect they showed your father.'
When the flame had come close enough for Berrigan
To call out to it, I heard him speak these words:

'You there, two souls trapped within one flame,
Perhaps you recall my face, for I was once
A visiting professor here, many years ago,

When I took over from Robert Lowell.
If you remember me, or remember my verses,
Which still stand on the shelves of the library,

Then speak to me now, and tell me, if there
Was ever a time when one of you, sailing the
High seas of scholarship, bit off more than you could chew.'

When Berrigan had finished speaking the
Greater horn of the ancient flame began
To shake itself, murmuring, just like a flame

That struggles with the wind, then, flickering
At the top, as if it were the tongue that spoke,
Threw out a quiet voice, and said:

'When I'd done my third stint as HoD,
A job that by then I could do in my sleep,
I set my sights on loftier goals.

Neither the thought of retirement in the
Yorkshire Dales, nor the debt of love that I
Owed Susan, could quench my thirst for knowledge.

The British Academy had launched a new funding
Round, aimed exclusively at those with a
Good track record, encouraging A-list scholars

To break new ground, going beyond the
Merely interdisciplinary to develop
New synergies between the disciplines.

Our project was bold, and stretched the available
Expertise of a department already
Weakened by maternity leaves, retirement,

Cuts, and the relentless expansion of
Creative Writing – but its combination
Of rigour and flair gave it a sporting chance.

We called it Project Darwin, and its aim,
Put crudely, was to retrace the voyage
Of the *Beagle* from the Cape Verde Islands

To Mauritius, with a team of experts,
And developing talent, from a range of
Disciplines: Biological Sciences were central

As was the Centre for Latin American Studies,
But the crew included travel writers,
Historiographers, cartographers,

Representatives from Myth Studies,
Art History and Philosophy, and colleagues
Working in the History of Science.

Inevitably, with restrictions on
Humanities funding tightening by the hour,
Our bid failed – the cruiser alone would have cost

An estimated £6,000,000 – but
We didn't abandon our idea altogether.
Cutting our losses, we borrowed the VC's yacht,

And I set sail with a group of colleagues,
Not many, who had not deserted me.
We could see the shore until we passed Tenerife,

Then we struck out from the Cape Verde islands,
Leaving all land far behind us, for days on end,
Till at last we sighted Bahia, where we took on

Fresh provisions. From here we stuck to the coast,
Leaving Rio de Janeiro and Montevideo
Behind us. We were old and tired academics,

Not used to the rolling of the ocean.
"Colleagues," I said, "you've sat through departmental
Meetings nearly as long as this voyage,

And much duller; but if you're short of things to do
This is as good a moment as any to check
Your Course Material Repositories.

And as we near our goal, don't forget why we came here,
You're Essex men and women, not sea dogs,
And you're here to pursue paths of excellence and knowledge.

The next RAE is only round the corner,
And for the humanities it's time to sink or swim."
I could not have known how prophetic my words were to be.

As we rounded the cape a tempest rose from the west
Striking the fore-part of our yacht. Three times it made
Her whirl round, at the fourth it made the stern rise up,

And the bow sink down, till the sea closed above us.'

CANTO XXVII

By now the flame was straight and still,
It spoke no more and began to drift away
From us, with sanction from Berrigan,

When another, that came behind it,
Drew our attention to its tip
With the strangled sounds that issued from it.

As a torture victim, shut in the romper room,
Will let out cries of pain as the Prods
Set about their sectarian DIY,

But because his mouth is strapped with
Insulation tape, the voice remains muffled,
So the dismal words here seemed eaten up by the flame.

Yet just as the voice will grow clear when the tape
Is ripped off, so now the words, having found
Their way to the tip of the flame,

Which gave them outlet like a tongue,
Became audible, and we heard it say:
'Did I hear you talking in the voices

Of the living? If so, and if you
Have recently descended from the sweet air above,
Tell me, is Northern Ireland at war or at peace?

For I was once curate at Cullion,
Near the village of Desertmartin.'
I was still leaning forwards, trying to tune in

To his wavelength, when Berrigan touched me
On the shoulder and said to me:
'You speak to him. He is of your land.'

And I, who was unprepared for my speech,
Leant further still towards the burning flame,
And said: 'Spirit, flickering below in the pit

Of flames, the land of which you speak is not,
And never was, without war in the hearts
Of its zealots and paramilitaries,

But since the Good Friday Agreement
The guns have quietened down,
There is no open conflict as I speak.

Yet in much the situation has not changed.
Rogue IRA units still assassinate
Catholics in the RUC and plant car bombs,

And only recently the Queen's visit
Was threatened by a bigot in a balaclava
At the 1916 Memorial

At Cregan cemetery in Londonderry.
And every year on the twelfth of July
The battle lines are drawn up fresh.

Today the city on the Lagan lies as ever
Between tyranny and freedom,
As it lies between the mountain and the sea.

And now I ask you to tell me who you are,
And to speak as freely as I've spoken to you,
So may your name on earth keep its flame burning.'

It flickered a while
Shifting the sharp point to and fro
And then blew out these words:

'If I thought for a moment I was talking to
A fellow who might return to the world
This flame would shake no more;

But if what I've heard is true, nobody
Has ever returned alive from this depth,
So without fear of infamy I answer thee.

I was a Republican and a priest,
Believing that the dog collar was the perfect
Cover for my misdemeanours:

And, to be sure, I was right enough,
Till that interfering High Priest showed up,
May his soul be damned!

Let me tell you exactly what happened.
While I still wore the bones and the flesh that
My mother gave me, my deeds were not those

Of the lion, but of the fox.
I was a dab hand at the fundraiser,
Bingo, dances, gymkhana, you name it,

I even set up a wee radio link now and then
So those who weren't there could still be part of it.
When the event was over, I'd tip off the boys,

And they'd make off with a fair share of the loot.
We were robbed so many times at these events,
That rumours began to circulate,

People started to say things, but
There was nothing anyone could prove.
Nonetheless, I thought the time had come,

As it comes for every man, to tighten
The rigs and pull down the sails, but little
Did I know what lay round the corner.

It was then I was approached by the High Priest.
The ceasefire had broken down, and he wanted
Something to take the heat off the fighting in Derry,

The dog collar I wore was of no concern.
As Constantine once sent for Sylvester
To cure his leprosy, so this one implored me.

"What do you want from me?" I asked him,
Looking him in the eye. He shifted in his seat
A little, then said: "We need someone to

Deliver a few packages to Claudy."
I knew what he meant, straight away, and I
Gave him a look as if to say you must be mad.

Then he spoke again, saying: "The cause is good.
The Lord will forgive you. Afterwards, we
Can find a parish for you in the Republic."

Eventually, when his arguments had
Pushed me to the point where silence seemed
No longer to be an option, I said: "I'll do it,

But I don't want any dead."
It was around ten o'clock that we planted
The bombs, the place was busy with shoppers.

When we'd made our getaway, we stopped in
Feeny to make a call, but the phone box
Was out of order. We went on to Dungiven

And tried again in the shops, but it was
The same story, all the phones were out
Following an attack at the exchange.

The men told the shop assistants to warn
The police, but by now it was too late.
The bombs exploded, causing total carnage,

Leaving nine dead, Protestants and Catholics alike.
It was a day that haunted me for as long
As I lived, there was no peace for me after that,

Even across the border this horrible
Affair hung over me like a black cloud.
When the time came for me to meet my maker

I made confession to Father Liam,
I wanted to go to the grave with a clear conscience.
I was hoping to go to the other place

But the moment I died I was whisked down here,
Todd Landman greeted me with a knowing smile
And consigned me to this pit of flames forever.'

When his words had ended, the flame,
In sorrow, departed, writhing
And tossing its sharp horn.

We passed on, Berrigan and I,
Making tracks for Zone 8, Area I,
Where the bridge crosses the pit in which those

Who have sown discord pay Hell's tariff.

CANTO XXVIII

Who could, even in the goriest movie,
Tell the tale of blood and guts
That I saw now – no matter how he filmed it!

I guarantee you every effect would fail,
Our minds cannot deal with such terror
Beside which all representation must pale.

If one could pile up all the wounded
Who once on Vinegar Hill
Mourned their blood, spilled by the Brits,

And those from that long siege,
Fed on a diet of 'dogs, mice
                        and candles', as Kee writes,

And pile them with the ranks mown down
On the banks of the Boyne,
And with all the bodies left sliced apart

In heaps by Cú Chulainn, and add those
Torn apart by car bombs or letter bombs,
Conquered, weaponless, on the way to work –

If all these dismembered and maimed were brought
Together, the scene would be nothing to
Compare to Zone 8, Area I's bloody sight.

No wine cask with its staves all ripped apart
Gaped wider than this man I saw split
From his chin   to where we fart.

His guts hung out,
       I saw his lungs, his liver,
          and the coiled tube that turns all to shit.

While I stared at his inner organs
He caught my eye and with both hands
Opened   his chest: 'See how I tear myself!

See how the Reverend Ian Paisley is
Ripped asunder by his own bare hands!
And look over there, where my wee boy is,

He's not a pretty sight, not with his
Face cut up from his chin to the crown.
The sinners that you see here

Are all the same – we're the ones
Who in life tore everything apart with schism,
And so in death you see us torn apart.

A surgeon stands back there who trims us all
In this cruel way, and each of these wicked souls
Feels anew the sting of his scalpel

Every time we make the round of this sad road,
For our wounds have all healed up again
By the time we get back to his surgery.

But who the Hell are you, hovering by the bridge
Trying to wriggle out of the
      sentence passed on you?'

'Death doesn't have him yet, he's not here
To suffer for his sins,' answered Berrigan,
'I, who am dead, lead him from gyre to gyre

So he may see how it is in Hell.'
More than a hundred in that place stopped
Short, when they heard these words,

Forgetting, in their amazement, what they
Suffered, to gaze at me   a living freak.
'Well then, you who will see the sun,

Tell that Gerry Adams that he'd better
Get the Fenians to stop stockpiling arms,
Or he might just fall victim to a stray bullet.'

With the heel of one boot raised, as if to go,
Paisley spoke these words,
      then was off.

Another, with no legs, and his throat slit,
And his nose torn off
                    to where his eyebrows met,

Who had stopped to gawp like all the rest,
Stepped out of the group and opened up
His throat to speak:

'You there, who walk this path uncondemned,
Remember the face of Seamus Twomey
Who planted the car bomb in Donegal Street,

Killing six, and maiming more than the
Souls you see here. And tell those
Dealers from Bogside, Martin and Shaun,

That if our foresight here is no deception,
They'll be turfed off a yacht in Lough Neagh,
To feed the fishes, by a double-dealing crook.'

'If you want me to tell your story up above,'
I said, 'tell me now, who is that one without
Lips or tongue, who hides at your side?'

At that, he laid his fist on this one's hair,
Dragging him up for us to see, and cried:
'Here he is, and he is mute.

This civil servant stood at Thatcher's arm
And drowned her doubts: he swore that men who
Are prepared to fast should be prepared to die.'

How helpless and confused he looked,
His tongue lopped off as far down as the throat,
This curio who once spoke with such assurance.

Then one who had both arms, but no hands,
And no ears,
                    raised his stumps in the air

And cried: 'No doubt you remember
Michael McKevitt, who refused to
Give up the bloody struggle, and took

It to the streets of Omagh!'
'A botched job,' I replied, 'which spelled
The end of you and your thugs.'

And he, this fresh wound added to the others,
Went off like one gone mad from pain.
But I remained, to watch the crowd,

And saw a sight I could hardly credit,
A body with no head that shuffled along,
Moving no different from the rest.

He held his severed head up by its hair,
Wielding it like a lamp,
And as it opened its eyes it spoke:

'See my despair!' When he arrived
Below the bridge on which we trod,
Halfway to the Data Archive,

He held the head up high, to let it
Speak from nearer by. 'Examine
Close my monstrous punishment,

And see if you find suffering to equal
Mine. I am Oliver Cromwell, who
Showed the Irish my hard steel,

And severed the head of King Charles.
For this I carry my own head
Forever cut from its life-source.

In me you see the punishment fit the crime.'

CANTO XXIX

The many souls and their crippling mutilations
Had made my eyes so drunk with horror
That they longed only to stay, and weep,

But Berrigan said: 'What are you gawping at?
Are you going to stand there all day ogling
These wretched mutilated shadows?

You weren't like this in the other Zones.
Now hold on, if you want to count them, one by one,
Remember, the Essex coastline

Is 350 miles long.
We haven't got that much time to play with,
And you've still got plenty to see.

'If you knew the reason I was sticking around,'
I said, 'then maybe you'd understand,
And let me stay a little longer.'

But already Berrigan was making tracks.
I followed close behind him, trying to
Get him to listen: 'Look,' I said,

'In that pit where I kept my eyes so fixed,
There's a dear shade belonging to my own family,
Who was stabbed in the chest by a shithead dealer.'

Then Berrigan spoke: 'There's no point dwelling
On past wrongs, what's done is done.
I saw the one you speak of, he was standing

Beneath the bridge, dressed in sportswear,
With blood all over his chest, and seemed to
Beckon you, like the ghost of Hamlet's father.

I even heard the other shades calling him:
Finn Western Davey – but you were staring at
Cromwell all the while, and he went off.'

'Bollocks,' I said, 'his violent death, aged 23,
Which is still fresh, has yet to be atoned for,
The shits who were involved got off lightly,

And are unrepentant. I guess that's why
He went off without addressing me,
And that only makes my sorrow the more.'

We chatted on about this until we reached
The other end of the bridge, by the Data Archive,
Digital double of Al's Bulge,

And its last outpost,
From where we saw into the final pit,
And with more light could have seen to the bottom.

Wild shrieks and lamentations pierced me,
Like arrows whose tips had been barbed with pity,
So that I put my hands over my ears.

Imagine all the diseased in the hospitals
Of Baghdad, Tripoli and Kaboul,
Between the months of July and August,

All flung together in one ditch;
Such was the misery here; and the stench
That came out was that of rotting flesh.

We passed the bridge's end to where a solitary
Bench stood, at the top of a grassy bank,
From which viewing point

One could see quite clearly into the depths.
I doubt the misery of the Indians
Who died in their hundreds

During the siege of Fort Pitt,
When Trent gave the Delawares
Two blankets and a handkerchief from the

Pittsburgh smallpox hospital, as a gift,
Was greater than the sorrow I beheld of the
Souls languishing in heaps in that dim valley.

One used a corpsed belly for a bolster,
One lay with his head crushed into another's
Shoulder, while others crawled aimlessly

Along the tarmac track. Step by step we went,
Without speech, examining the sick
Who could not raise their bodies.

I saw two sit leaning against each other,
Like book-ends in a library closed down by
The cuts, covered from head to toe with scabs.

I never saw a chisel applied by
A porter, who has been called to
Break into an office with a broken lock,

Struck with more force than those two used,
Clawing themselves with their bare nails
To find release from the terrible itching.

They worked their nails down under the scabs
The way Keith Floyd used to wield a knife
To de-scale a bream for a fish supper.

'You there,' began Berrigan, 'scraping off
Your mail shirts with your fingers' ends,
Like Edward Scissorhands,

Tell us, are there any Americans
Hanging about in this ditch?'
'We're Americans,' one of them spoke back,

Through eyes that wept salt tears.
'But who the Hell are you, walking tall
Amongst these dudes you see disfigured here?'

And Berrigan replied: 'I'm a shade, like you,
Who, with this living man, goes from pit to pit,
And I mean to show him all of Hell.'

At that, they sat up straight, and turned
To stare at us wide-eyed, and the heads
Of many another in the ditch looked up too.

Berrigan came up beside me and whispered
In my ear: 'Now it's your turn to speak.'
Then, since he wanted me to take over,

I said: 'Tell us who you are, and where
You're from, so that your stories may
Live on in the world you have left behind.'

'I'm from Kansas,' one of them replied,
'I got blown out of the air by friendly fire
Patrolling the no-fly zone over Iraq.

We were out on a mission,
Flying above the cloud layer, high on
Adrenaline, Napalm Death on the headphones;

The two of us you see here
Thought we might put the wind up our
Squadron leader, we were just goofing around,

Like we were in *Top Gun*; so, we dived on him,
Like we would if we were hostile,
Meaning to pull off at the last minute,

And I guess we kind of left it a little
Bit late, so he opens fire with two Exocets,
Blows us right out of the skies, *kppowww!*'

And I said to the poet: 'They don't come
Dumber than the Americans. Even the
Irish are no match for them.'

'Watch your lip, dude, or I might just crawl out
Of this ditch,' the other one snapped,
'You've obviously never metten an Iraqi.'

Then, as if to prove his point, he began
To reel off a string of jokes:
'Question: What should Iraq get for its air

Defence system? Answer: A refund.
Question: Why doesn't Saddam go out drinking?
Answer: Because he can get bombed at home.'

Berrigan was looking more and more pissed off
With his countryman, as one gag followed another
In an endless stream. 'Shut the fuck up!' he said,

Swinging a boot at him. 'It's you and your
Kind who have dragged our flag through the mud.
We're out of here.' At that he turned,

And began to climb once more up the bank.

CANTO XXX

According to myth, Juno was once so
Enraged against the Thebans over Semele,
That she made King Athamas go insane,

So insane, that when he saw his wife
Stepping towards him, with a child in each hand,
He cried out: 'Spread the nets,

That I may trap the lioness and her cubs
At the pass!' And then he spread out his
Crazy hands as if he were the net,

Grabbed one of his sons and battered his brains
Out against a rock. She drowned herself
                    with the other one.

And when Adam Ant, fresh out of the nuthouse,
Thought someone was threatening his daughter,
He lost it completely

Put a brick through the window of
The Dick Turpin, and pulled out a blunderbuss
(For he is a keen collector of antiques);

As the police dragged him off, now out of his mind,
They say he began to howl, like a dog.
The thought of going back inside snapped his mind.

But never in Thebes or London did you see
Crazies as ferocious as the two naked shades
I saw now as I looked back into the ditch:

They charged about madly like wild boar
When hunted, snarling and snapping
At anything in their path.

One, crashing into the comedian,
Fixed his incisors on his neck-joint, dragging
Him off so that his belly was flayed by the tarmac.

Trembling, where he now sat alone, the Kansan
Cried: 'You see that crazed spirit? That's Jonny Saatchi.
He used to do impressions in the SU Bar,

Then he earned a tidy sum sitting
Exams for the Chinese. He's rabid!'
'And what about the other one?' I asked.

'Shit,' he said, 'you don't want to know.
That dude came here as a mature student
To study Biological Sciences,

Under Professor Pretty. He was a
Hardened drinker who got so wasted one night
That he shagged his own step-daughter,

She was in Myth Studies, a girl half his age.'
When the rabid pair, on whom I had kept
My eyes fixed, had run off

I shifted my gaze to look on the other
Ill-born spirits;
I saw one, a woman, shaped like a lute,

Except that she still walked on legs,
Like some creature out of Hieronymus Bosch.
Bloated by booze

Her body's parts were disproportioned
By unconverted toxins,
So that her face was all shrunken and petite,

While her belly stuck out like a wide shelf,
Or like the prow of a ship,
And her swollen lips were folded back,

Parched and wide apart,
As those of a creature suffering from
A raging fever, craving a drop to drink.

'Hello,' she said, 'what are you doing here,
Do I know you? And why are you walking
Around without any affliction?

I can't think why you should. Hey?
Look carefully, and see the misery
Of Elaine Jordan. When I was still living

I had enough of what I wished. Ah!
And I don't regret it at all, not for
One moment. But look at me now –

I crave one drop of water!
The little streams that run through the fields
In Dedham Vale, towards Willy Lott's Cottage,

I can't get them out of my head, they haunt
Me, making me like one of those worried spectres
In Tennyson's poetry. Do you read Tennyson?

Those waters, their memory makes me far
More parched than this wasting disease.
I can still see Wivenhoe, where I learned

To get up at the crack of dawn
To shuffle up to the Co-op – that hill! –
So as to feed my habit.

Ah! If I could find those wretched dons
That taught me, making me dream,
So that I stayed up all night.

The misery of it. If I could lay my hands
On them, they're here somewhere, I'm sure of it,
But these legs of mine won't go far.

If I could cover a couple of yards a day,
And thought they were ten miles away,
I'd be off. But I can't even manage that.'

'Tell me,' I said, 'who are those two spirits
Lying supine beside you,
Steaming like wet gloves in wintertime?'

'These two? They were here already when I
Tumbled into this ditch, they haven't stirred
Since and I doubt they ever will.

One of them is John Coombes, he's so lazy
He never even bothered to turn up to
His own lectures. He was always

Finding some excuse to skive off work,
Leaving the poor students in the lurch,
Even in their final year. The other one

Was the Dean, a gifted linguist,
But not a real worker like me.'
Then one of the pair, perhaps disgruntled

By the introduction he was given,
Suddenly sat up and struck out with his fist
At the rigid belly. It sounded like a drum.

Then Elaine Jordan took a swing at him
With her arm, catching him on the jaw
With equal force, saying to him:

'Though I can't get about like I used to
I still have a steady arm when required!'
To which he snapped back: 'But it wasn't so steady

When you used to go out on the piss, was it?'
'Get your hands off me, you old prophet!'
She yelled. 'Go back to sleep!

You think yourself some grand academic,
But where are all those books you promised?
You're nothing but a sham!'

I was engrossed in their wrangling
When Berrigan tugged me by the shoulder,
Saying: 'Leave off,

You don't want to get tied up in these old
Quarrels, you should know better.'
When I heard the anger in his voice

I turned scarlet through shame.
I felt like one in a dream,
Caught in a situation I wished to be out of,

Who, still dreaming, wishes it only a dream –
But I was not dreaming. 'Forget it,'
Said Berrigan, 'you don't need to go there.

But if you meet up with this sort again,
Slagging each other off while Rome burns,
Just remember, I'm here for you. To develop

A taste for this kind of talk is dangerous.'

CANTO XXXI

The same tongue that spoke in anger – stinging
Me so that blood filled the capillaries in my cheeks –
Supplied the Savlon for my wound,

Just as, or so I have read in old books,
The lance bequeathed to Achilles by his father
Could heal the injuries it inflicted.

We turned our backs to the wretched trench,
Climbing to the top of the bank which girds it round,
Then we crossed back over the bridge

And Berrigan led me across the square
And out of Zone 8 into Zone 9,
Whose border was marked by a pole bearing a sign.

'These poles,' said Berrigan, 'serve a double purpose,
For in the event of fire or other emergencies,
They serve as Assembly Points; this one serves

The Lecture Theatre Block, and some of the labs.'
As he spoke, he pointed out the labs
With his finger, then added:

'When the alarm goes off it's something else –
Because it has to be heard over the voices
Of the scholars delivering their lectures

And since, in addition, it has to be sure
To wake up any students who have dropped off
It has a special sonic frequency

Which can penetrate concrete and the thickest skull.
The technology was pioneered right here
On this campus, they call it Roland 2.'

It was pretty dark where we were standing
And as I cast my eye about in the gloom I
Seemed to see a host of giants closing in

On us. 'What's up with Goliath and Co.?'
I asked, and Berrigan, my guide, said:
'You've got it wrong, partner, these aren't giants,

They're towers; the original plan was to
Include a lot more than there are now
As well, but let's get a little closer,

So you can see for yourself.' As when
Dry-ice lifts, the eye little by little reshapes
What till then the air-crowding vapour hides,

So, as my eye pierced that darksome air,
Drawing closer to these edifices,
My confusion began to clear too.

Just as at Montereggione, the
Round wall is crowned with high towers,
So the round hill here was dotted with tower blocks.

'Here,' said Berrigan, 'you see the ambition,
But ultimately, too, the failure, of
Modernism – the uniformity

And functionalism first advocated
By the likes of Le Corbusier,
The so-called "international style",

See their apotheosis in these towers.
But as Jencks later saw, these
Monstrous structures were ultimately

Uninhabitable – they filled up with
Low-lifes and drug users until the point
Was reached where they had to be given the

Coup de grace by dynamite –
Which as Jencks puts it marks the death of
Modernist architecture.'

As we drew close to one of the towers
I could make out one of the faces at a window,
A student who appeared to be off his head,

And as we passed by he cried out
What sounded to me like total gibberish:
'Rafa! Maya! Make me shabby! All me!'

'That dude,' said Berrigan, 'kind of makes the point.
He's like Nimrod, the one who built the Tower of Babel;
After the building of that structure

He lost the power of speech, just as the earth
Lost a common tongue – of course, that's just myth,
But it kind of explains one of the problems

With the modernist block – the overwhelming scale
Ultimately leads to a breakdown in
Communication amongst communities.'

We strolled on along a rising track
Until the towers lay behind us,
Then I saw up ahead a low circle of

Buildings, built from pale brick, with little
Balconies overlooking an area of grass.
They were brighter and much less

Intimidating than the towers I
Had mistaken for giants, and I asked Berrigan:
'Who lives within these blocks, are they reserved

For the graduate students, or visiting
Professors? They certainly look like
An improvement on the towers.'

'Those are the South Courts,' he said, 'I think
Anyone can stay there – it's just a lottery
Whether you end up here or in the towers.

But you're right, apart from the building work
That's still going on, which you'll see in a minute,
It's a more user-friendly place to live – in that sense,

As well as the nod to past architecture,
I mean, it's a bit like a Georgian crescent,
It represents a more postmodern

Approach to building in Jencks' sense:
It's what he calls double-coded, at once
Old and new, popular and elitist.'

We kept on walking all this while,
And by the time Berrigan had stopped talking
We had arrived at a security gate,

Which blocked our path. A notice in red
Stated: ANTEUS SECURITY:
RESTRICTED ACCESS. Berrigan went up to

The window of the Portakabin:
'We're on a campus tour,' he said, 'we'd like
To visit Zone 9, Areas A–D.'

'Sorry mate,' came the voice from within,
'Authorised personnel only.'
'This trip has AHRC funding,' said Berrigan,

'And Dean's approval.' 'That's what they all say,'
Said the security guard, 'I'll need to
See your ID if you claim you've got clearance.'

Berrigan handed him some documents
Which he began to leaf through suspiciously.
'Is this one living?' he asked, sounding surprised.

'Sure is,' said Berrigan. 'Well, that's a first!'
Said the guard. He began to type something
Into his computer, and Berrigan lit a smoke.

Eventually, he looked up, smiling, and said:
'You're in,' at which point the gate clicked open
And he took us inside, handing us a couple

Of hard hats. 'You'll need to put that cigarette
Out, guv'nor,' he said, 'inflammable material.'
Berrigan took a last, long drag, then stubbed it

On the ground, as the guard led us towards
The edge of a huge pit dug into the earth
In the centre of the ring of flats.

'It may just look like a massive hole in
The ground to you, mate,' he said, 'but this
Here is the future of student accommodation.

When it's finished, there'll be a whole city
Down there, Cocytus Campus we call it,
All the flats come with wi-fi and *en suite*,

And the whole lot's carbon neutral as well.'
We were now standing at the yellow
Barrier which circumnavigated

The rim of the pit. Peering over the edge
I could see nothing, so deep and dark it seemed;
'If you're wanting to go down,' the guard said,

Pointing at a kind of cage on a pulley,
Like those used to clean the outside of glass buildings,
'This is the only way. I'll leave you here.'

At that Berrigan fastened his hard hat
And stepped into the unsteady contraption,
Pulling me in beside him. The guard shut the gate,

Then pressed a button. Slowly we began our descent.

CANTO XXXII

If I had stanzas rough and jolting enough
To describe our descent
Into this pit hollowed out of the earth

Whose walls supported the converging weight
Of Hell, then I would press the juice of
My memory to the last drop.

But I don't have them, so balk at going on.
To describe this heart of darkness as it truly is
Is no child's play, no place for jingling lines

That come off pat. I doubt those ladies that
Helped Amphion wall in Thebes
Can be of much help.

As we went down, unsteadily,
Scraping against the compacted layers of
History, Berrigan handed me a snow-suit.

'You might be needing this,' he said, 'put it on.'
We hit rock bottom as I was pulling up the zip,
And as I stepped out, dizzy, still gazing up at those

High walls, I heard a voice address me:
'Mind where you step, big fellow, you don't want
To be crushing the heads of these sorry souls

With your big boots.' At once I turned around
And I saw stretching before me and beneath
My feet a vast lake, frozen over,

So that it looked more like perspex than ice.
Even those freak winters cold enough to freeze
The Colne over from Wivenhoe to Mersea Island,

Or to freeze over the waters of Lough Neagh,
Never made ice so thick as you saw down here;
If Slieve Gullion had been dropped on it,

Or even Slieve Donard, it wouldn't have cracked,
Not even at the edges. And as frogs sit
With their bodies half out of the water,

Croaking away, in that season when academics
Put their feet up, brushing up on Gramsci,
Or concocting a new reading of *Paradise Lost*,

So these shivering shades were wedged in the ice,
Right up to their belly buttons, their teeth
Chattering away like joke-shop dentures.

Every one of them held his face pointing
Downwards, like politicians browsing in a porn
Emporium, their teeth testifying to their

Suffering, their eyes to the sorrow in their hearts.
When I'd had a good look around, I glanced
Down at my feet, and there I saw two shades

So pressed together that the hair on their heads
Was entwined. 'You there,' I said, 'who won't let
Each other go, tell me who you are.' At this,

They twisted their stiff necks, and when they had
Raised their faces towards me, their eyes,
Which were bloodshot with the cold,

Began to shed tears, which fell to their lips,
Freezing fast as they went so that the two
Were ever more firmly locked together.

An industrial stapler never fixed
Plasterboard to wood so strongly;
And they, like dodgems, constantly bumped each other.

Another one, who had lost both ears to the cold,
His face peering into the icy mirror,
Called out: 'What are you staring at?

If you want to know who these two are,
The valley where the Bann descends
Belonged to them, and to their father Brian

O'Brien, an Ulster Chieftain; they fought over
Their inheritance till both lay dead.
And let me tell you, if you search the whole of

Cain's Corner, you won't find souls
More fit to be stuck in this frozen aspic;
Not she who beheaded her cousin Mary,

Not Jack Wall, who stabbed his brother after
A day's drinking, not even this one here
Whose head blocks my view, Sean MacHeron:

His family ran a removals firm in
Carrickfergus where he murdered his cousin,
Burying him in concrete, to get his hands on

The business; if you're a northerner, you'll no doubt
Know the tale. And to save you the trouble of
Asking, I'm Seamus O'Connol, who quarrelled

With my uncle over a farm; my crime
Was nothing compared to my cousin Owen's,
Who told the Brits we were storming the castle.'

Afterwards, I saw a thousand doglike faces
Made purple by the cold, and I thought of
The pub at the top of Scheregate Steps,

The Purple Dog, and wondered if its owners
Had visited this region of Hell.
That's why I shudder, and always will,

Each time I walk past it, and rush by
The man selling *The Big Issue* there.
While we made our way farther into the

Frozen Zone, crossing the ice with careful steps,
Perhaps it was fate, perhaps chance, I don't know,
But picking our way through the heads,

My Docs struck one of them in the face.
Letting out a yelp, it barked at me:
'What the Hell do you think you're doing!

Surely you haven't come to punish me
For fetching the English across the water?
For Christ's sake, lay off!' And I:

'Berrigan, my master, wait here a moment,
I'd like to check this one out, then
We can press on as quickly as you like.'

Berrigan stopped dead in his tracks,
And I turned to that purple shade,
Who still hadn't let up cursing, and said:

'Who the Hell are you, losing your rag at us like that?'
'I like your sauce,' he answered, 'what on earth
do you think you're doing marching through here

Kicking people in the head? Not even a
Living man could kick as hard as you do!'
'I am a living man,' I said, 'and if you

Know what's good for you, tell me your name,
So I can put you in my notebook
And spread your fame at the Writers' Forum.'

'Not likely,' he said, 'that's the last thing I want.
You've got a funny idea of flattery.
Now bugger off and leave me alone!'

Then I grabbed him by the scruff and said:
'If you want any hairs left on your head
You'd better give me your name.'

'You can tug away till I'm bald,
And kick my teeth in for all I care,' he said,
'I'm giving neither name nor number!'

I already had his hair twisted round my
Fist, and had pulled out a few handfuls,
As he kept up his howling,

When another voice cried: 'What's up, Dermot?
It's bad enough listening to your teeth chattering,
Do you have to start barking as well?'

'So it's you,' I said, 'Dermot MacMurrough,
The biggest traitor of the lot! I might have guessed.
I'll make sure I tell about you, don't worry.'

'Fuck off!' he answered. 'Tell what you like,
But if you're lucky enough to escape this hole
Don't forget to mention that blabbermouth

Russell: "I saw," you can tell them, "the bastard
Who stood by as the Irish dropped dead through hunger,
Stuck up to his neck in the fridge."

And if anyone asks you who else was there,
Right under your feet is Billy McCaughey,
And if you go on a wee bit, you'll find that

Turncoat Florence MacCarthy, along with
MacMahon and Gerald Fennell who would have
Opened the gates at Clonmel while the people slept.'

We had already left him, when I saw
Two frozen in one hole so close together
That the one head was a cap for the other,

And as a famished man sinks his teeth into
A crust of bread, so the uppermost sank
His teeth into the brain of the lower.

If old books carry any truth, this must
Have been how Tydeus gnawed the severed
Head of Menalippus in his rage.

'You,' I shouted, 'you on top, what fury
Makes you suck the very marrow from that
Meat, what hatred feeds your appetite?

If you've good reason to take such revenge,
Tell me what it is, and I will repay
Your trust, repeating your words in the world

Above, if my tongue doesn't dry up first.'

CANTO XXXIII

Raising his mouth from that horrible snack,
This blood-soaked shade wiped his lips clean on the
Squashed thatch of that head he had chewed up behind

Then spoke: 'You've got a cheek, wee man, asking
Me to rake over the coals of a grief so desperate
That the very thought of it freezes my bones;

But if my words are to be a seed, that may
Bear the fruit of infamy for this traitor
That I gnaw, then prick up your ears,

For you shall hear me weep and gas at once.
I've no idea who you are, nor what business
Brings you traipsing around down here, but something

In your voice tells me that you were once from Belfast.
Know then, that I was Bobby Sands, and this
Here is Maggie Bloody Thatcher – now let me

Tell you why I am so unneighbourly.
Maybe I've no need to tell youse that it was her
Government that locked us up with common criminals,

Denying us political status
When there was a war on. But the cruelty of
My imprisonment you can not imagine.

When they took away our fucking clothes, we went
On the blanket; when they emptied our chamber pots
All over our fucking beds, only then did we

Start our dirty protest. The stench was appalling,
The cells were literally covered in shite,
And everywhere you looked there were flies and maggots.

It was like something out of Dante, like,
Only this was really happening, in 1979.
Through the thick pane of frosted glass

I'd gazed on many passing moons, when I
Woke to the banging of truncheons on perspex.
Before you could say "Up the IRA!"

We were ripped from our cells and dragged along
The corridor by our legs, then we ran the gauntlet
Of the ranked riot police who hit us with

Truncheons as we passed; we were kicked and
Pushed to the floor, where they pinned us down,
Then sheared us like sheep, scrubbing us

With floor mops, before they tossed us back inside
Our cells. They had done their best to break us,
And had failed, when at last they seemed to give in

To our demands – but it was a lousy trick,
The clothes they offered were not our own.
We trashed the place screaming blue murder,

Vowing revenge on the whole pack of them.
The next day we sat in silence, and the
Day after that as well.

It was around the time they brought our food
That the idea came to me, it had
Worked in the past, so why not try it again?

Hunger Strike. But this one would be to the death,
Each striker starting at intervals, and each time one
Of us died, another man would step into his shoes.

It's no joke watching yourself die like that,
The pain is indescribable
As you start digesting your own innards –

Anyone but the immovable Thatcher
Would have compromised before ten men died,
But all she said was "A crime is a crime is a crime.'"

When he had spoken these words he rolled his eyes
Like a famine victim, then seized the miserable
Skull with his teeth, which as a dog's were

Strong upon the bone. Oh Long Kesh, blot
Upon the landscape of that fair country
Where the sound of 'aye' is heard!

So what if Bobby Sands bombed the
Balmoral Furnishing Company,
Did that give you the right to make him

And nine others die before letting the
Politicals wear their own shirts?
The greatest betrayal in politics is retrenchment,

And the British Government's inflexibility,
Matched only by the inflexibility of the hunger strikers
Themselves, prolonged the conflict by 20 years.

We made tracks to where the frost encases
Another pack of shades, not bent downwards
But fixed gazing up.

Here the very weeping puts an end to tears,
And the grief, which cannot find release through their eyes,
Turns inwards like desire in hysteria,

For their first tears formed a frozen knot
And, like freezing eye-packs, filled up
All the cavity beneath their eyebrows.

It was so cold that all feeling had been driven from
My face, my lips were numb, like skin that has
Hardened to form a callus,

Yet even so, it seemed to me I felt
A wind getting up, so I asked Berrigan:
'What's the cause of such a wind,

I thought no heat could reach these depths?'
And Berrigan replied: 'Just be patient, soon
· Enough you'll see for yourself the cause of this blast.'

They must have heard us talking, for one of the shades
With their eyes buried beneath the crust
Cried out as we passed: 'You wretched sinners,

Sunk so low that you've been given the last post!
Remove the hard veils from my eyes,
That I may give vent to my grief a wee bit,

Before the tears ice up again.'
Then I told him: 'If you want me to give you
Some first aid, first tell me who you are,

And if I don't help you afterwards
May I be sunk forever beneath the ice.'
He answered then:

'I am Gerald Barry, I was given life
For murdering Manuela Riedo, a Swiss student
On vacation in Galway, in 2007,

Then they gave me life again, even though I
Pleaded guilty, for the rape of a French student
A couple of months earlier.'

'Oh,' I said, 'and you're already dead?
Didn't you serve your sentence?'
And he replied: 'Just what my body's doing

Up in the world I couldn't tell you,
But I'll let you in on a secret:
This isn't the only corner of the campus

Where you'll find a fellow who hasn't yet
Popped his clogs. And just so that you'll be
All the more wanting to peel the ice-flows

Off my face, let me tell you, when a soul
Behaves like I did, a demon takes over the
Body, controlling it like a zombie

For all its remaining days on the earth,
While the soul drops straight into this cistern here;
And that smarmy Baptist wintering out

Behind me, he may well be up on earth still,
For all I know, perhaps you could tell me,
If you've just come from there: he's the

Baptist dentist, Colin Howell, who bumped off
His wife and his mistress's husband,
Then staged their joint suicide in a car

In Castlerock. He's been down here so many years
I've lost count.' 'But that can't be so,' I said,
'I've heard about this case, it was only recently

He confessed, after a crisis of conscience,
He's only just started serving time.'
'That may well be,' he said, 'but believe me,

The souls of Lesley Howell and Trevor
Buchanan had not yet reached the muddy shore
Where Dr May greets the freshers before

The dentist left a zombie in his place
At the surgery, and the same goes
For his accomplice. I swear to you,

That's God's own truth. But enough of that,
Lend me a hand as you promised, open
My eyes.' I did not open them.

To be rude to him was courtesy itself.
Ah, Londonderry! You've bred so many
Fucked-up fanatics it's a wonder God

Doesn't wipe you off the map, for I found
One of your men, consorting with Galway's worst,
Who for his foul deeds bathes already in Cocytus,

But his body seems alive and is serving time amongst you.

CANTO XXXIV

'Now put your goggles on,' said Berrigan,
'We're going into Zone 9, Area D,
The Judas Precinct as they call it,

You'll see why soon enough.' As he spoke
I peered ahead through the freezing mist,
Which now blew fiercely into our faces,

And in the distance I could make out
What looked like a huge underground wind-farm,
Though the blades were spinning faster than

Any I'd seen before. 'What's with the
Wind-turbines,' I said, 'why would you put something
Like that underground?' 'That,' said Berrigan,

'Is no wind-farm, it was developed by
People in Computer Science to simulate
Arctic weather conditions – the idea was

To reverse global warming, and they thought
The device might have military potential too,
Like their Robotic Fish, you know, kind of

If they won't do what you want, put their whole
Country into deep freeze. If it had worked, whatever
The ethics, they'd have made a fortune, but they

Couldn't get it to function outside lab
Conditions, too many variables in the end,
Though it's highly effective at creating

The freezing conditions down here, which they
Need to preserve the Biological Archive.'
'The Biological Archive?' I asked.

Berrigan knelt down and began to scrape
Away the layer of frost that covered
The ice, and as he did so I saw that

Beneath the surface were souls fixed in this
Frozen element (I tremble as I write it in verse),
They looked like flies trapped in an ice cube.

Some of them were lying flat, some stood upright,
Some were suspended upside-down, others,
Like gymnasts, bent their heads towards their toes.

'Look,' said Berrigan, 'that one standing on
His head is Enoch Powell, who gave a talk
Here in the sixties; beside him,

In the military garb, is Dr Inch from
Porton Down, an army research base which
Had links with chemical warfare –

It was his visit which sparked the student sit-in
Which once made Essex notorious.
If you look closely beneath the ice

You can still see a few groups of students
Sitting around – they'll sit there till doomsday
Waiting for their demands to be met.

Further down still, though so far down you'd be
Lucky to catch a glimpse of them, are the
Politicians who made war on countries

They'd previously been happy to sell arms to –
Some of them you might recognise, like Blair and Bush,
Others are buried so deep you'll never spot them.'

'Berrigan,' I said, 'why do all these people
Suffer together here, I mean, what do they
Have in common? The students' cause was just,

From what I know about it, they were fighting
To stop one of their fellows from being expelled
For heckling a fascist.'

'That's true,' he said, 'like any archive, what's
Collected here, at the end of the day,
Is a pretty mixed bag, but one thing that

Links all these people together on a
Technical level is the betrayal of
Benefactors:

Blair betrayed those who'd voted him into office
By going to war with Iraq, the students,
Whatever the rights and wrongs of their cause,

Betrayed those who fought to get them a free
Education, and ultimately put this
Right in jeopardy; Powell,

Whose crime is the worst of all,
Betrayed a whole generation
                              of immigrants.'

I don't know how long we crouched, gazing into
The ice, but by the time we stood up my
Back was aching. 'This way,' said Berrigan,

'There's another part of the archive I want
To show you.' As we advanced into the cooler
We reached a point where our path began to

Descend, and on each side a wall of ice
Rose up. When the path levelled out again
We stopped for breath, for now the wind had dropped,

And looking round I found myself in what
Looked like a maze of corridors carved into
The ice. 'The Archive of Dreams,' said Berrigan.

He reached out his hand, touching the wall,
And pulled out a vertical sheet of ice,
Which slid out like a drawer. Looking closely

I could see that it had a text carved
Into its surface. 'Read it,' said Berrigan,
'Or pick another one. This is where all the

Dreams of staff and students who have been
At Essex are stored, there are billions of them.'
As he spoke I pulled out another sheet of ice

On my left and, squinting, read out its contents:
'In my dream I was racing with the VC down
A long corridor. We both rode penny-farthings.

The faster I pedalled the slower I went.
At the end of the corridor lay my pension.
As we approached it seemed to get further

And further away. When we finally got
To it there was nothing left except a
Pre-decimalisation ten-shilling note.

"I win," said the VC. (Gender: Female.
Member of: Staff. Age range: 36–45).'
'OK,' said Berrigan, 'now we must go,

We've seen it all.' So saying he took my hand
And led me down a corridor on the right
Which was dark and endless. At last

We came to the head of a metal staircase
Which descended in a spiral, and as we went
Down I grew dizzy. 'Hold fast!' said

Berrigan, 'For by such stairs must we depart
From so much ill. The way is long, and difficult
The road.' I was hot and sticky by the time

We reached the bottom. Berrigan kicked open
The door and we stepped out into the stinking
Service area once more, making our way

Past the bins and the cars and the litter,
Choking on the fumes which came from Hell's kitchens,
Till we came to a point from which we could

Once more see the clear light of day.
We took off our snow gear, throwing it
In a skip, and crossed the road,

Stepping straight onto a number 62.
It was crowded with students going home
From class, we couldn't find a seat for us both.

Then, as we pulled out, Berrigan began
To tremble like a heatwave
                    and vanished.

The girl beside me was reading her stars.

INDEX

Liam, Father, 118
Libya, 102
LiFTS (Department of Literature, Film, and Theatre Studies), 32
Limbo, 6, 15
Lion Lion, 82
Literary agents, 102, 105
Lough Neagh, 122, 139
Logbook, 16
Logos, 72
London, 129
Londonderry, 21, 116, 148
Long Kesh, 146
Lopez, Tony, 16
Lowell, Robert, 16, 112
LTB (Lecture Theatre Block), 110, 134
Lucca, 88
Lucky Strike, 34
Luncheon vouchers, 88

MacGowan, Shane, 59
Maeve, Queen of Connacht, 20
MacCarthy, Florence, 143
MacHeron, Sean, 141
MacMurrough, Dermot, 143
Mahler, Gustav, 92
Maldon, 53
Malory, Sir Thomas, 22
Manganese, 29
Mangan, James Clarence, 59
Marketing, 19
Martin, 122
Mary, Queen of Scots, 141
Matisse, Henri, 66
May, Adrian, 11, 148
McCaughey, Billy, 143
McDonagh, Siobhain, 17
McKevitt, Michael, 122
Memorial Day, 5
Menalippus, 143
Mendelssohn, Anna, 44
Mersea Island, 53, 139
Mills and Boon, 103
Modernism, 135
Monroe, Marilyn, 20
Montereggione, 135
Montevideo, 114
Morrison, Blake, 109
Moss, Roger, 62

Mothballs, 90
Motion, Andrew, 104
Movement, the, 105
MUD1 (Multi-User Dungeon), 18
Muldoon, Paul, 7
Musselwhite, David, 111
Mystic Meg, 84
Myth Studies, 113, 130
Myxomatosis, 1

Napalm Death, 127
Narragansett, 85
Negative equity, 79
New American Poetry, 67
New England, 84
New York, 66, 68
New York School, 16
Nichomachean Ethics, 47
Nimrod, 136

O'Brien, Brian, 140
O'Connol, Owen, 141
O'Connol, Seamus, 141
O'Connor, Hazel, 105
Oedipus, 111
Okri, Ben, 18
Oliver, Douglas, 16
Oliver, Jamie, 89
Omagh, 123
Orangemen, 25, 92
Orford Merman, 93
O'Shea, Kitty, 24
Oulipo (*Ouvroir de littérature potentielle*), 5
Ovid, 108
Oxbridge, 10
Oxford, 104, 110

Paisley, Reverend Ian, 120
Paolo, 88
Paradise Lost, 140
Phaethon, 74
Philosophy, 113
Pisspants, 90
Pits, the, 78
Pittsburgh, 125
Plante, David, 68
Plasterboard, 140
Pogues, The, 60
Porton Down, 150